Trust Your Increments

Praise for *Trust Your Increments*

An invaluable book, filled with colorful stories about mastering the rules of the old boys club while climbing to the top of the corporate ladder. *Trust Your Increments* had me taking notes, nodding my head, and laughing out loud. It's so rare to have a female leader as powerful and honest as Laura share her secrets. A must read!

> **-Keltie Knight,** *New York Times* Bestselling author, three-time Emmy winner, CEO and co-founder of The Lady Gang, and executive producer of CBS's *Superfan*

Trust Your Increments challenges each of us to think about our personal mission and focus on what matters most, rather than living an aimless life. It's a creative blueprint for anyone looking to maximize their potential and achieve ambitious career goals by taking small, yet consistent steps in the right direction.

> **-Ron Douglas,** *New York Times* Bestselling author

The data is very clear on the funding gap for women entrepreneurs, women led businesses, and even women leadership in large organizations. I believe the roots of this issue are so deeply embedded in our culture that they are difficult and complex to address, often having to peel one layer away at a time. I do believe it is about overall mindset and taking it one step at a time. Kudos to Laura for diving into this topic to help contribute to bridging this gap!

> **-Nicole Verkindt,** tech entrepreneur and investor, Startup Canada Women Entrepreneur of the Year (2017, 2019)

Laura Casselman was a small-town girl, turned Radio City Rockette, who now runs an award-winning international technology company. She's a shining example of where there's a will, there's a way. Laura sets goals and crushes them while having a bit of fun along the way. If you're interested in climbing the corporate ladder or starting your own company, Laura Casselman is the one you want to learn from. Period. You will be happy that you placed your trust in her.

-**Melinda Martin,** CEO of High Level Strategies, self-made multi-millionaire

Leading isn't easy, but Laura is a leader unlike any other I've met in my life. She is directly responsible for helping me create an eight-figure business. The chance to learn how to find your passion, thrive at it, and achieve your life goals is one not many get . . . but one you WILL learn from *Trust Your Increments.* If you are wanting more out of life, *Trust Your Increments* is the perfect place to start.

-**Luke Maguire,** eight-figure founder of Social Media Mansion, recipient of "40 Under 40" Top Entrepreneurs Business News Australia

I've proudly styled Laura for six years, and I am thrilled to see her sharing thoughtful tips and tricks to inspire others in the business world. In a few short years, she has conquered the unimaginable in this male-dominated world of tech and entrepreneurship, and I believe she will be a household name! Grab this book, share it with other like-minded women, and get ready to soar in every aspect of your life!

-**Emily Loftiss,** national television personality, lifestyle expert, personal stylist, and founder of wildly popular "Everyday Glam Gazette," a monthly newsletter known as "Goop-for everyday people."

Laura is such a kind soul and incredible human being to look out for! She's got her heart in the right spot, and I can't wait to see what magic she will continue to create!

-**Jasmin Manke,** 7-figure CEO, Forbes "30 under 30," international speaker, and success mentor for entrepreneurs

Written by an amazing leader, *Trust Your Increments* is packed with wisdom and solid growth systems and can only add huge value to your life!

-**Andrew Fox,** co-founder of Zapable

Get access to the **result accelerators** included with your purchase of this book!

Inside you'll find . . .

◇ How to **ace a job interview** cheat sheet

◇ Instant **confidence boosters**

◇ **How to ask for a raise** flash cards

◇ The **ultimate Slack hack**, copy & paste messages.

◇ Personal interviews with **leading entrepreneurs.**

And much more...

Unlock Your Result Accelerators Here

Step 1:	**Step 2:**	**Step 3:**
Go to: trustyourincrements.com/setup	Create a free account & use your bonus code	Login to access all your bonuses

TRUST
YOUR
INCREMENTS

How Small, Consistent Steps Can Lead to Massive Success

LAURA CASSELMAN

NEW YORK

LONDON • NASHVILLE • MELBOURNE • VANCOUVER

TRUST YOUR INCREMENTS

How Small, Consistent Steps Can Lead to Massive Success

Published in New York, New York, by Morgan James Publishing. Morgan James is a trademark of Morgan James, LLC. www.MorganJamesPublishing.com

Proudly distributed by Ingram Publisher Services.

A **FREE** ebook edition is available for you
or a friend with the purchase of this print book.

CLEARLY SIGN YOUR NAME ABOVE

Instructions to claim your free ebook edition:
1. Visit MorganJamesBOGO.com
2. Sign your name CLEARLY in the space above
3. Complete the form and submit a photo
   of this entire page
4. You or your friend can download the ebook
   to your preferred device

ISBN 9781636980058 paperback
ISBN 9781636980065 ebook
Library of Congress Control Number:
2022941517

Cover Design by:
Alex Radisic
design@vidastreet.com

Interior Design by:
Chris Treccani
www.3dogcreative.net

Morgan James is a proud partner of Habitat for Humanity Peninsula
and Greater Williamsburg. Partners in building since 2006.

Get involved today! Visit MorganJamesPublishing.com/giving-back

For my daughter, Dagney.
May you never settle for what someone else says
you're capable of becoming or worth being paid.

Table of Contents

Introduction

E verything you've been told about climbing America's corporate ladder is outdated and just plain wrong!

Sure, most boardrooms are full of old white male dinosaurs . . . and the few women who managed to fight their way to the top are often worse than their male colleagues.

The good news is that you don't need to strap chainsaws to your elbows to make it.

There's room and a great need for more good people at the top.

In this book, you'll discover the fifteen small and incremental steps you can take to become a force for positive change . . . and to climb the ladder without compromising your personal values.

Sure, sexism does exist. In fact, it's quite rampant, and some of my personal experiences are guaranteed to shock you.

As a woman, you will get paid less than your male counterparts. You've heard the number 82 cents on the dollar, and that may not sound too bad. However, that is the average. The hard reality is that if you are a Latina woman, you'll only be paid 55 cents on the dollar.

You will experience the "innocent" office banter that's nothing but poorly disguised sexism.

You will be passed over for jobs and promotions due to your gender, and during interviews you will be asked questions about kids, pregnancy, and family they would never dare ask a man.

Of course this all needs to change, and thankfully, we are slowly moving toward a better, fairer, and more equal future for women, people of color, and good people in general.

My goal with this book is to empower you with the tools you need to climb to the top, without selling your soul or compromising your values. It will teach you:

- How to get paid what you're worth
- The power of the word *no*
- How positivity leads to change
- How to find confidence
- How to focus on what you do well

And once you start applying these fifteen powerful incremental changes to your career, my hope is that you won't just make it, but also that you'll use your influence to bring about more positive change.

The best thing that could happen is that this book becomes obsolete in ten years, when there are no longer women or minorities in business and we're all just people in business!

This is my personal story of how I went from being a small-town girl with big dreams to becoming CEO of a multi-billion-dollar tech company in a male-dominated industry.

It's about my years as a Radio City Music Hall Rockette, how that led me into the NYC boardrooms, and how I made it back down South as the CEO of a big company with a more modern, inclusive, and progressive stance on leadership and business in general.

It's not a pretty story, and it definitely has more villains than heroes.

That said, it *is* a story about good people, about sticking up for your values, and about having a positive influence on America's corporate culture and board rooms.

Now, even though my career has been riddled with horror stories of blatant sexism and downright disgusting episodes of male chauvinism (one of them was so bad my dad drove cross country to "save" me!) . . . this is *not* a #MeToo book.

As important as that battle is, I'll leave that to other people.

This book focuses on telling it as it is—the good, the bad, and the ugly, with the aim of giving you some fifteen incremental steps you can use in your career starting today!

These actionable steps will help you avoid the worst BS, get paid what you're worth, be treated fairly, and, not least, to succeed on your way to the top without selling your soul.

Because unless we get more good people in the boardrooms, nothing will ever change!

> **That next good person could be you!**

If you flip to the next page, you'll see how your success journey starts with two things: liking yourself and finding confidence in your abilities.

The rest is simply a series of simple steps, and as you're about to see . . .

If the door is closed, I'll find an open window for you!

Chapter One

I Like Myself

My name is Laura Casselman, and I am a woman in business. I feel that I should get that out of the way early, in case there is still any confusion. *Why* I should have to announce such a thing is another chapter for another time, as is what being a woman in business actually *means*.

Am I supposed to wear a red power suit complete with three-inch shoulder pads like an extra from *Dynasty*? Am I expected to preface every comment or suggestion I make in a meeting with, "Speaking as a woman, I feel . . ." as opposed to simply offering insight as the CEO of a software company? Am I letting this side down by failing to lock myself in the bathroom stall to cry for several hours each day? When do I stop being a woman in business and start being a successful businessperson?

Let's hold that thought for now though. The facts remain, I am Laura Casselman, and I am a woman in business. There's another fact that I'd like to share, though, and it's one that some people

2 | TRUST YOUR INCREMENTS

find a little hard to swallow. I *like* being Laura Casselman. I *like* being a woman in business. That's right—hold onto your hats—*I like myself*, and I feel confident in who I am.

It never fails to astonish and amaze me how many people seem to dislike themselves. I just can't fathom it. Forgive me for being blunt here, but we live in a world where people will wait in line to bring you down. Whether that's disillusioned coworkers, judgmental family members, or even embittered strangers on the internet, there will never be a shortage of people waiting to tell you that you're wrong and you should apologize for existing. Why in the world would you do their work for them? Don't you have enough on your plate?

Confidence Is Key

Confidence is so important to everything we look to achieve in our life. I worked hard on maintaining my own confidence throughout my life, and that's what has made me the person I am today. I'm not infallible, though, and my own self-belief has been rocked in the past. Life has a way of humbling us all, and I am no exception. My mind plays just as many tricks on me as yours; it's just a matter of how you handle those tricks and quieten down those nagging voices.

Let me give you an example. Before I entered corporate America, I was a fitness model, dancer, and sometimes, singer. Believe me, that can be a cutthroat world to live in! There's one audition that I'll never forget. I was sixteen years old, and I was auditioning for my biggest part yet. There was a twelve-year-old girl there, and when you're a teenager, those four years seem like an insurmountable age difference. If you're thirty-six and you speak to somebody who is thirty-two, there will usually be no discernible difference between you. When you're sixteen and on the cusp of adulthood, however, you're convinced that you know everything (you don't) and that this kid should be at home playing with dolls. (She shouldn't have been, as I was going to learn!)

Anyway, this girl knew that she wasn't old enough to successfully audition for the part and she couldn't be hired. She was just there looking to gain a little experience ahead of time. That in itself is a hugely admirable decision. It takes confidence to put yourself out there and surround yourself with older, more experienced heads. The auditioner was describing a particularly difficult dance move during the audition, and she explained that nobody could pull off the technique to perfection except Mikhail Baryshnikov. If you're unfamiliar with the dance world, that's arguably the most famous ballet dancer in the world. This twelve-year-old—who, lest we forget, my teenage mind had written off as a kid playing in a grown-up world—stepped up and pulled it off to perfection. It turns out that nobody could perform that move correctly except Baryshnikov—and Cameron Adams.

I felt so small. We were from the same area, and I was older, and by default I was supposed to be better. I stayed for around another twenty-five minutes, but I felt my confidence shrink smaller and smaller. Eventually I walked away—and to this day, that's the only audition I walked out on. I was in my own head, playing games with myself, and that meant that I wasn't paying attention and learning from the opportunity.

Now, hindsight is 20/20. Cameron Adams is still dancing on Broadway as I write this. She made her debut in *The Music Man* when she was seventeen and was most recently in *My Fair Lady*. That alone blows my mind. She's only four years younger than me, but I don't feel that my body could cope with it! It's her life, though, and she is so incredibly talented. Looking back, I think of how lucky I was to know her. I got to watch somebody at the top of her game, and learn from her, because she had a talent that I didn't. I was talented—performance was my life for eighteen years—but she was genuine, next level.

That whole experience taught me not to be envious of what other people had, but to learn from them. These were great people to ask questions. She may not have been able to explain everything exactly. It was just something that she could do; that's how talent works. She could at least break it down for me a little, though, and I could learn from that.

> **Why be intimidated by greatness when you could otherwise be inspired by mediocrity?**

There's a lot more of the latter than the former.

It's the same in the business world if you're passed over for a promotion that you think you deserve. Sometimes you do deserve it, but other times somebody else just has a skill set that you don't possess yet. Note those all-important three letters—*yet*. None of us knows everything, but we all have the capacity to learn.

Never Be the Best in the Room

I remember one of my previous jobs in New York City. I worked with a woman that was called a "shark in heels." As a sidebar, I know that's intended as an insult (not least because people said it about me too!), but I find it to be a mixed metaphor. Sharks keep moving or they die. Can't the same be said about people, as we grow and learn? Sure, we shouldn't replicate *all* shark behaviors—human resources may get involved if you start biting and eat your coworkers—but we could learn something about perpetual motion from them.

I digress. People would say of this woman, "She'll close any deal, but she'll sell her mother's soul to do it." Everybody hated her, but I got to know her, and she was quite brilliant. She was direct, and she made it clear that she wasn't going to tell me all her secrets. Why should she? She was generous though. She would invite me to meetings, and I learned from her and took things from it, things that I could adapt and put my own spin on.

I'm a firm believer that wherever you are and whatever you're doing, there should be somebody better than you. If you're the best in the room, what is there to learn? What are you gaining? Are you evolving as an artist, a businessperson, or a human? How boring would it be if we were the best at everything?

Maybe it's my background in performing arts that helps me remember that everything comes out in the wash. I may not have won role A because I was blonde, but being blonde may have been a deciding factor in me winning role B. Now, obviously business doesn't work that way. It's not OK to refuse to hire somebody because they're too short, have green eyes, or—whisper it quietly—are female. Performing arts helped me realize that there is enough of the pie for everybody to get their slice though. Rejection is like water off a duck's back for me.

I honestly believe that we can all get what we want, and there's no need to sabotage or trample over anybody else to get it. You just may not get it when, or how, you want it. When you're faced with a setback, you have to avoid dwelling on negativity and self-pity. That's not saying that you can never be negative. It's like with a break-up. There have been times in my life when I've allowed myself a night to drink wine, cry, and watch *Bridget Jones's Diary*. When the sun comes up, though, it's time to put on my big-girl panties and deal with whatever life wants to throw at me. Guess what—I'm still standing. Failure can be an incredible lesson, especially when you learn how to get past it. Nothing is permanent.

Forget the Rest—Focus on What You Do Well

I think it's a real shame when people don't really understand where their strengths lie. I think it should be mandatory for everybody, and it's the first piece of advice I would ever offer anybody: find what you're good at, and double down on that. I'm a talented dancer, and I have a good head for business. Give me a wrench and a leaking faucet, however, and I'll likely end up soaking wet and with a bigger flood than I started with.

I'm OK with that. I have enough confidence in myself to know that what I do, I do very well. In that scenario, I'll call a plumber. They won't go home and beat themselves up about failing to nail a triple pirouette, and I don't expect them to. Likewise, I'm not going to lose any sleep over the fact that I can't do everything. That's just not realistic.

Stop worrying about what everybody else is doing.

The only person that you're in competition with is yourself—
the you of yesterday, last week, last year, ten years ago.

Just keep moving forward, keep evolving and keep learning. I had a quote from the author Daniel Hillel on my wall throughout my dance career that said, "I get up. I walk. I fall down. Meanwhile, I keep dancing."

That really struck a chord with me, and it's how I promised myself I would be every night that I was on stage. That's life too. If you fall down seven times, just get up eight. You're still winning!

It's just about focusing on the right part of failure. What can you learn from it? And, look, sometimes even the most colossal failures are hysterical! It pays to look back once the dust has settled and have a good laugh. I was sitting in a café once, and I saw this guy trip. He was trying *so* hard to style it out and make sure that nobody noticed, and it made me realize something. Every time I trip—and, yes, it happens, even trained dancers fall on our butts—I laugh hysterically. I just don't care. I'm a human being—it happens. I trip, I stub my toe, I spill my coffee. Focus on the parts that we can learn from, and if we can't, just have a good laugh.

Never Apologize for Being Confident

One of the drawbacks of being confident is that some people bristle at your sheer audacity in refusing to second-guess yourself. On the other hand, some people are encouraging about it. As always, it's a matter of surrounding yourself with the right people.

Personally, I have never been ashamed of where I work. I think that earning an honest living is something to be proud of, and if you contribute to this world, that's awesome. I don't care if you have a college degree—having a trade or skill is every bit as admirable to me. Some people may call that blue-collar, and that's cool. I just think that everybody who contributes deserves to be recognized and respected for their skill and effort.

I remember that I interviewed at a local Walmart when I was a freshman in college. They wouldn't hire me because, in their words, I was too ambitious. They said they didn't have time to train me when I'd just leave in a few years. I explained that I would be committed for at least those few years, but they were adamant. That was fine—I was honest with them, and they were honest with me in return. That was the first time that somebody had told me I was too ambitious.

Later, when I was working in New York, I was working for a manager that I really respected and learned a lot from. Every year, when I returned from touring with the Radio City Rockettes, I would get a promotion and move up a tier. When we first started working together, she was way above me in the corporate hierarchy. After about three years, though, I was just beneath her. Suddenly, I was a threat in her eyes.

I didn't see myself that way. As far as I was concerned, she was a few years older than me and had more experience, and I just wanted to continue learning whatever I could from her. She thought I was gunning for her job though. Every time we were in the same room, she would be abrasive with me. She walked into my office for a meeting once and said, "Oh, you should have the power seat." I was fine sitting on the other side of the desk, and told her that! It ended with her telling me that she knew I was gunning for her job. I said before that there is enough of the pie for everybody, and I meant that. She wasn't in a singular position; she was one of about eighty district managers.

Was district manager my next career move? Yes, absolutely. Did that mean I wanted to oust her, like some kind of corporate Lady Macbeth? Of course not. People move on all the time in business. They retire, they change companies. I was prepared to wait for a vacancy to open up, and keep on learning in between. She was glad to hear that I wasn't gunning for her job, but she never trusted me after that. I ended up interviewing for a district manager role at another company and took the job there instead. Sometimes you just have to pick and choose your battles. Immediately she reached out and asked if there was anything she could do to help me—it was so clear that she was relieved that I was leaving!

It's like I said before, competition with ourselves does not have to be competition between our peers. We can all get ahead without trampling on anybody else in the process. The way I look at it, I was this woman's hire. She took me on, and I learned from her. The fact that I was making progress was a testament to her teachings. It just seemed that she thought she had reached the ceiling of her own potential and that the only way for her to go was down. I never want to feel that way. There's always a chance to learn more and do more.

If the Door Is Closed, Find a Window

A resume in the world of business is like a headshot in the world of performing arts. It will get your foot in the door. That's it though—it will get you into a room, but it won't keep you there.

> The line between confidence and misplaced arrogance can sometimes appear to be a thin one, but it's hugely important to learn how to stay on the right side of it.

Take an interview situation as an example. If somebody is interviewing you for a job, you'll need to explain what you can bring them based on your skills. That's not arrogance—that's just stating important facts. In addition, though, people have to like you! If you're going to be sharing an office with this person, they'll probably see more of you than their spouse or kids. Chemistry is essential in that case. If they can't stand the sight of you after an hour, how do you think they'll feel after a busy week at work?

Even an unsuccessful interview is a great opportunity. Write to the people you met, thank them for their time, and ask them if they have any advice for you in the future. Now, we live in a litigious society, so don't ask why you didn't get the job. They won't touch that question and may consider it best not to reply at all. Asking for advice though—what you could have done better, what would help you during your next interview—can be really helpful.

Many times, they may still just say you did a great interview and leave it at that. That's happened to me, and in these instances I circled back to an individual. I sent them a personal message saying that I enjoyed meeting them, that they asked some great questions, and asking if they would be willing to meet for coffee to offer some advice as it would be hugely important and beneficial to me.

Some people may clear their schedule for lunch and have a good, long conversation with you. Others may only be able to spare ten minutes. If that's the case, make those ten minutes count! You can achieve a lot in that time span. Anything you can learn to improve will get you one step closer to where you want to be. This tenacious spirit also conveys confidence. These companies may not be hiring right now, but they will be again in the future. They'll remember you if you show a willingness and eagerness to learn. That immediately puts you half a step ahead of the competition, who are approaching the situation more passively.

Ultimately, there is no substitute for shaking somebody by the hand and looking them in the eye. You can learn a lot from books and webinars. Showing that you're not discouraged by not getting the job at the first time of asking though? That's something that will stick with an employer. Even if you don't end up working with these people, keep them updated on your progress. Tell them about what courses you've taken and where you're working. That's how you'll find that fabled window that you can climb through while everybody else is lining up outside the door!

Of course, none of this matters unless you're confident in yourself. Confidence is not unlike a reputation—it can take a long time to build and can be torn apart quickly. Learn how to inflate a bubble of confidence and self-belief around you, and focus on what you know you're good at doing. Perhaps most importantly, you do you and stop comparing yourself to others. As Oscar Wilde so memorably said, "Be yourself—everybody else is taken."

Chapter Two

No, I Am *Not* Your Equal!

I made a rookie mistake the other night. It had been a good day, and I was feeling pretty relaxed. I was all set to call it a night, and then I did something a little silly. I logged into Facebook.

I know, right? I brought this on myself. I don't lack self-awareness.

Sadly, it appears that I can't say the same for some of my peers. A post that announced that women are faking sexism in the workplace confronted me, and I immediately went from feeling pretty good about life to despairing at how this line of thinking still exists.

I'm pretty sure you don't need to be told that it was a man that posted this. It blows my mind that he felt confident enough to say it though. I would accept such a statement from a woman. I may not *agree*, but I'd be able to accept that she had her own personal experience to draw from. A man though? He hasn't walked in my shoes, and I don't just mean because they wouldn't fit him.

It's akin to me informing people of color that there is no such thing as racism in the United States from my position as a white woman. I can say that *I'm* not a racist, but I cannot say with any degree of sincerity that they will not be treated differently because of the color of their skin. They are. It's an uncomfortable fact, but it's a fact all the same. It would be *cute* to hear men talk as though they know something about what life is like for women in corporate America, if it wasn't so dang frustrating!

#KillAllMen? No Thanks.

I want to make one thing clear before we go any further—**I do not hate men**. In fact, I love good men, and I make a point of keeping them in my life. I am not speaking *against* men when I speak *for* women. I'm a firm believer in the classic, traditional meaning of feminism—that women should be treated fairly and equally. I don't think that means that a woman needs to be involved in every male thing. You want an all-male university? Cool. Have an all-female university too.

I have changed my Instagram to explain how I empower women—but that doesn't mean that I'm tearing down men. The only post I have ever made that even mentioned men was one that said, "A woman without a man is like a fish without a bicycle." I got a whole lot of private messages from men after that, telling me that I needed to tone it down and think about how I was appearing.

I just don't understand why they were so upset! It had nothing to do with them personally, or men in general. You can inflate one group of people without deflating another. There's enough air for all of us if we share. Didn't we learn how to do that in kindergarten? All the same, I was told to consider how I was coming across, so I considered it. I can't quite recall what I did for the rest of the minute, but I'm sure it upset somebody.

I think there is definitely something sinister about the approach of some men in the workplace, but a lot of it is cultural. We have grown up with sexism toward women in the workplace, and it was allowed to become the norm. That's why I say that it's now time for everybody to educate themselves—men *and* women. When I saw that post on Facebook about the women faking sexism, I wished that guy would have taken a breath before hitting the button and taken a moment to look into the situation.

There are numerous occasions when I let things slide. I just think, "Look, it's a man of a certain age; he doesn't know any different." I'm not happy about it, but sometimes you just have to pick the hills you're prepared to die on. It's like dealing with a stubborn child. If a young child is insistent that the sky is green and grass is blue, you're not going to change their mind and get them to respect your point of view. All you can do is move on and hope they see their mistake sooner rather than later.

Men Are from Mars, Women Are from . . . a Slightly Different Part of Mars

Speaking from my own perspective as a woman that has climbed the corporate ladder, I can honestly say that I have never had a job in which I was not sexually harassed or mistreated due to my gender. I want to make one thing very clear at this point, though—it hasn't only been by men. My female bosses intentionally placed me in bad positions for their own gain, as they knew they would look better if I got a sale or finalized a deal.

I once had a female boss set me up for a dinner meeting. So far, so standard. I got there, and it was pretty much immediately clear that this was not work related. I called her to find out what the heck was going on, and she told me that this guy was the mortgage broker of her home property, and it was my job to ensure she got a favorable rate.

I was furious. I was a professional, and she basically pimped me out. I'll be honest, I doubt she got the rate she wanted, as this mortgage broker did not get the night he was expecting! I told him up front that we were having dinner and the night would end with me getting into *my* car and returning to *my* home—alone. I made it clear that *he* was footing the bill, as I was not using my corporate expense account. Why would I? It had nothing to do with business.

I knew that I had to play by the unwritten laws of the game. I wasn't supposed to make waves, and I wasn't supposed to go to HR about what had happened. I just had to bite my tongue until I reached a position of power where I could change the rules myself. Well, that's where I am now, and I ensure everything I do is fair to all sexes!

Women Belong in the Business World Too

Everybody deserves to be comfortable in the workplace. I don't care about your gender, age, sexual orientation, or whether you consider Nickelback to be the greatest rock and roll band of all time. As a CEO, my responsibility is to ensure the people who work for me do not feel threatened or undermined.

Let's take workplace humor as an example. A certain element of society loves to complain about politically correct culture, claiming that nobody can say anything anymore. There's a time that off-color jokes work for everybody and everybody is laughing along. That's great! We all need to laugh sometimes, even if it's gallows humor, or we'd bang our heads against our desks and cry. If somebody feels uncomfortable, though, we need to find out why.

The culture of my company is relaxed. We laugh and joke all the time—it's not an uptight place to work. However, there have been times that people have approached me and said that they feel uncomfortable about a situation, and in my opinion they were correct to feel that way. Let me be clear, though: my opinion here isn't what matters. Protecting my employees is!

In fact, I have felt that way myself many times in my career. Once a shareholder, in front of a room full of paying customers, asked me to do the splits. How does that play into my ability to do my job? I thought that bending over backward for the customer was supposed to be a metaphor? He just wanted to degrade me and suggest that I didn't have a brain, so everybody should see what I could do with my body.

Maybe it's because of my background in performing arts. If you want to assume that because I am proud of my performance background that I can do nothing else, then that's your lookout. Karma is a wonderful thing, and you'll learn that yourself eventually. I just feel that anybody who spends any period of time with me will quickly realize that I not only have a brain, but also I use it. That means that I deserve to be paid the same as any man who does my job, and yet, that's not always the case.

Steer Your Own Ship

Whether an employee is male, female, or anything in between, I try to do for others what I wish others had done for me—but equally, I hold employees to the same standards I hold myself to.

I don't micromanage, and that's hugely important to me. There is a supplier that we work with that has fewer customers than JVZoo by about half, but they process the same turnover as us because their service is more expensive to use. We have fifteen employees; they have over three hundred. That, to me, looks like a whole lot of middle managers. I don't understand why that is necessary. Executives should always be evaluating their teams and what exactly each person on their team is doing to contribute to the company. Far more often than not, departments are overloaded with freeloaders and space fillers.

Those are the people who I always had an issue with because they were just creating processes for the sake of justifying their own salary, and blocking me from receiving my next raise. I was doing the work to get the company where it needed to be. These employees were standing over my shoulder, watching me do that work. Why? What was that achieving? I'm either an adult that is doing the job I'm paid for, or I'm not, and you can fire me. That's my personality.

I have learned that it's not a personality everybody shares. Maybe it's a generation gap. I pay attention to market research that explains how younger employees want to know they are changing the world through their work, and they are constantly filling in surveys about how they *feel* about what they are doing. Our CIO is also a lecturer, and he has brought in employees he taught at university. We'd bring them in as interns and hire them, but sometimes they learned they needed a micromanager.

That's fine, and I suggest that they clean up their resume and find a business that provides that. I'll give them more time as a notice period, as I appreciate them coming to me with this revelation, and I'll gladly help with a cover letter, but JVZoo is not the environment for them. Nobody here believes in micromanaging, and I'm not your mom! Speaking of which . . .

Baby? Maybe

We are still two hundred years behind equal pay for women, and that just blows my mind. How can we still be penalizing women for giving birth, or even the very threat of giving birth due to their age? Employers are thinking, "What am I going to do when this person needs time off?"

As a CEO of a company our size, I am not legally obligated to offer maternity pay. I do, but I am not mandated to do so. We have plenty of moms working here, but we just recently had our first person fall pregnant while employed by JVZoo. We had to think of things as a whole new ballgame.

I'm a CEO, so I have to look at the bottom line—that's what I'm paid for. That, and doing the splits in front of customers, apparently. I knew that I had to find a way to pay for somebody else to cover this employee's workload while she was off, but I wasn't going to penalize her for it!

I gave her 6 weeks off on full pay, which is more than the average of 4.1 weeks in America. She asked me if she could come back sooner if she wanted to, but I had to laugh. I told her that she would be welcomed with open arms, but I doubted she would want to take up that opportunity!

Naturally, when those six weeks elapsed, she wasn't quite ready to return. She'd had a complicated birth, and her baby was sick, so it was a really tough time. We eased her slowly back into things, changing her hours and letting her find a solution. Remember, we don't micromanage our employees. We firmly believe that adults can work things out for themselves.

One thing we would *not* do is reduce or penalize her paycheck, or pay her any less than a man. She had a burden that her husband could not meet. If this world is going to keep spinning, women are going to have to give birth. What's more, she would come back and do her job much better than a new employee because she knows what she is doing!

I have seen so many of my female friends almost have their careers ended by pregnancy though. They were expected to start over from the very bottom rung of the ladder, punished for the sin of bringing life into the world. They have had to start over at the bottom in a new industry because they are not prepared to do that for a company where they had already fought their way to the top.

What's in a Name?

I work in a male-dominated industry. Tech is male-dominated to begin with, and when we factor in the digital marketing industry, we're looking at maybe 98 percent testosterone. This means that, to this day, I am addressed by nicknames that are intended to belittle me.

People send me emails saying, "Hey, Barbie," which I find fascinating. I am the CEO of the company that you are asking for support! I'm not running a small company that processes a million dollars a year. I'm not running Google, either—we still have a way to go, but we turn over hundreds of millions each year, and I know exactly how much each of our customers makes. What makes those people think they can degrade me by calling me Barbie? Especially when they're asking a question they could easily answer just by clicking through our online knowledge base?

It seems that because I am a female CEO, people feel comfortable writing straight to me and asking me a question, prefaced with a nickname. I half expect to be asked for a recipe for apple pie while they're at it, seeing as we apparently still live in a world of 1950s gender stereotypes.

I'd like to say that it's just bravado from behind a computer screen, but sadly it happens at live networking events too. People who I know to be *good* people seem to refuse to look at me in conversation. I remember being at an event in California, where one of the major players in our industry just would not look at me or involve me in a conversation. Eventually another power user of JVZoo stepped in and introduced me.

At this point, the response was, "Oh my gosh, *Laura*? I just assumed you were somebody's girlfriend!" It was bizarre! I mean, this person has a female CEO at their own company—it's not like I'm a unicorn. Even if I was, was I really not worth being addressed or even looked at just because I'm female? Even if I was "just" a girlfriend, why assume that I know nothing about the industry and would have nothing to contribute to the conversation? I will say that the person in question apologized profusely and sent me a plethora of messages explaining how shocked he was by his own actions. I told him not to sweat it, because to be blunt, I'm used to it.

Is that not part of the problem though? Should women just *accept* this kind of treatment because it's ingrained in the culture of the corporate world? Situations like this are where things get very tricky as a female CEO. As it happened, I didn't *need* to be part of that conversation. I had my business year planned out already, and that guy wasn't part of it. In that respect, it was a case of no harm, no foul—let's all learn from this and be better people for the experience.

What would have happened if I *had* needed to network with him for business though? What if I had a revenue gap in my Q4 forecast and I needed to drum up some customers? The only way I could have done so would have been to forcibly interrupt and interject myself into that conversation. I have no problem with that. I'll put my hand out, introduce myself, say it's good to see them, and get down to brass tacks. Thankfully, that person would have been fine with that too.

Others though? Not so much. I would be labeled a witch with a b, a ballbuster, rude, obnoxious, and pushy. Who in the world did

I think I was, sticking my nose into business talk and interrupting a serious conversation? Look, I've said before, I'm busy—I don't have time for ballast and bluster. I like to be blunt!

Blurred Lines

I have said already that I work in a male-dominated industry, and I have touched upon some of the stereotypes that arise as a result of that. A common one is that I'll be in a board meeting full of men, and one of them will say, "Hey, Laura, can you minute this for us?"

Now, I have checked my business card, my resume, and my job description, and none of them mention that I am a secretary in addition to being a CEO. With that in mind, how about no! Sure, I'll take notes—for *my* use and benefit. That's how I do business. Three months down the line, when you claim that you didn't agree to something, I'll be able to flip to the relevant page in my notebook and explain verbatim what you said, because I'm a good notetaker. I know what I'm responsible for.

When I explain this, most people agree that it's a fair point well made. There is always one outlier that mutters under their breath that I'm being a witch with a b though. Well guess what?

> If being a "witch with a b" means that I'm not your witch with a b, then I'm OK with that!

The point I'm making is that if you ever stand up for yourself as a female, you're going to piss somebody off. Experience has taught me that this will happen anyway though. Some people will always be upset at being stood up to, and if they want to make it a gender divide, then that's their business. I figure it's better to be hung as a wolf than as a sheep—the end result is the same. Stuff like that doesn't bother me. I take it all with a grain of salt. It's just othering.

One thing that never fails to fascinate me, however, is how people assume that because they find somebody attractive, they cannot possibly be intelligent. Surely attraction is in the eye of the beholder? Despite this, across the board, it seems that if a woman is deemed attractive, she can't possibly be *that* smart.

Now, I won't ever be designing rocket ships for NASA. I'm just not that kind of intelligent, in that kind of arena, no matter how much work I put into it. All the same, I *have* put a lot of work and effort into learning how to do what I'm good at and doing it well. Just because I may also brush my hair and apply some lipstick before a meeting, it doesn't mean that I'm stupid! I am actually capable of retaining the information I need to run a successful business in addition to doing that. It's not like every stroke of a hairbrush dislodges a pivotal piece of information from my brain. I'm just putting my best foot forward.

Social media is another tricky subject to approach. I acknowledge that I am being looked at, so I have cultivated a consistent presence across all platforms. When I think of what happened to LinkedIn, though, it's a real shame.

LinkedIn used to be where business people could congregate online. It used to be, "This is where you do business, and Facebook and Instagram are the Wild West where anything goes." Now, though, LinkedIn is my biggest source of spam. It's just pitch after pitch, the vast majority of which are irrelevant to my business, and every fifth message is a man I have never met saying that we should meet for drinks as he'll be in my city soon. Now that's an impressive feat in itself, as I have intentionally avoided listing my actual city on my profile!

Again, I'm sure some women do the same to men. I don't know personally, as it isn't something I've ever done, but I would never be so presumptuous as to say that it's impossible. I do know, however, how much harder I have had to work than any man to reach their level of pay. Do people really think that leaves me enough free time to deal with this BS as well?

#MeToo

OK, it's time to discuss the elephant in the room—the #MeToo and #TimesUp movements. It may have started in Hollywood, but a whole raft of women from the corporate world have experienced their own moments too. I am no exception.

I remember when I first became an executive in the corporate world, working in New York City. My boss at the time stopped my direct deposit pay and insisted that I collect a check from him every two weeks. He always wanted to meet for lunch at a restaurant, and in NYC, many restaurants are located on the ground floor of hotels. Every time, he would casually mention that he had a room upstairs. I would say, "No, Mr. W., I'm not interested."

I'm kidding about who was involved, but I'm not kidding about how this happened—and I certainly wasn't kidding at the time either. On every occasion, he was met with a firm, no-nonsense, "No." This didn't seem to register, though, as eventually he felt empowered enough to say that he at least deserved a BJ for all his efforts when I collected my check from him.

I quit that day, because I had worked too hard to deal with that crap. Now, I'm not saying that this has never happened to a man on this planet. I'm sure it has. I'm prepared to bet that it has happened to a lot more women though.

Another example involves a time that I interviewed for a role in legal services. The interview was a washout, and I didn't even get past the gatekeeper. After the meeting, though, I got a call from the person I originally wanted to meet, saying he had been passed my information and was sorry he missed me and wanted to have lunch with me. When I got there, it transpired that the gatekeeper had basically told him he should ask me out. I had been summoned to a supposed work meeting to be checked out as a potential girl-friend, and I was *irate*.

In this instance, I had been judged and talked about based exclusively on my appearance, following what was supposed to be a professional meeting. There was no review of what I could bring to the table from a business perspective, or what new ideas I might have. I doubt any of that was even heard in the interview. You know the saying, "There is no such thing as a free lunch"? That was never truer than in this instance. That meeting was not paying my rent, and it was actively costing me time and money.

Probably the only occasion I have felt physically endangered at work was when I was a teenager. I was eighteen and working at a hotel restaurant. I had a male manager who was very hands-on with all the women. He would call for room service from upstairs and always ask that I bring it. That was creepy in and of itself, and when we factor in that I worked the restaurant and did not deliver room service, the ick factor creeps up even higher.

This guy always made me nervous, so I would say to the other girls, "I'm taking this up to room 237. If I'm not back in ten min-utes, come and get me." One night he got aggressive with me, and I was genuinely scared, so much so that I called my dad.

Now, this whole experience taught me two things. First, do *not* call your dad unless you need to. He was two hours away but was there in ninety minutes. All he said to me was, "Get in the car," before he went in, and I did just that. He didn't want me to know what was about to happen, and I didn't want to know. I'm pretty sure it wasn't just a firm but polite exchange of views about women's rights.

Second, I learned that I should never let myself get so far along into a situation again. I was physically afraid for my safety that night, and I have never compromised myself in such a way since. *Nobody* gets physically close enough to intimidate me. There are plenty of situations in this world that we can't control. This, however, is one of them.

Everybody needs to have their own firm, hard line as to what they find acceptable and what they don't. I mentioned earlier that I quit my job on the spot because my boss wanted a BJ in exchange for my paycheck. You have to know where your self-respect dictates that you won't take any more. It's hugely unfair that anybody is put in such a position, but we have to draw that line every single day.

I have had a male boss tell me that my career would be greatly impacted if I didn't do exactly what he wanted me to and laughed in my face when I said I was going to report him to HR. He ended up getting fired, for the record! I have had other occasions where I have approached a company's HR about harassment, and they have shrugged it off. Other times, I have just ignored it. I wasn't in any direct, physical danger, and I decided to keep my powder dry and pick my battles.

Know Your Worth, and Stop Giving Discounts

When I first started working at JVZoo, I always got the same response from the CEO at the time, when I asked for a raise. It was always along the lines of, "It's about time you came and talked to me about this."

He rewarded hard work and intelligence, and he never gave handouts. I don't know if he realized this at the time, but he was quietly and efficiently coaching me throughout that time. Sadly, women are conditioned not to ask—again, that's a fast track to being labeled pushy and difficult. This man is a good guy, though, and while he was never interested in talking about feelings (and really, neither am I), I think the fact that he has three daughters played into his decision-making.

I have taken this approach to salary on myself as CEO of JVZoo. Ninety-nine percent of the time, I don't offer an employee a salary. I tell them to name what they think they are worth, and from then on it's down to them to earn it. You set the bar and jump to it every day. I'm not going to motivate you to do so—that's your business, and I have a company to run. Just tell me what your bar is, and jump to it every day. Fail to do so, and I'll let you go. That's fair, right? When I'm employing a woman, I often take them to one side after a while and say, "OK, here's where you went wrong."

I have one particularly educated employee. She has a PhD in computer science and twenty years of experience in business. She's also a mother of five. This woman is busy! When she was negotiating her salary, she told me her husband's salary, and she wanted $3K more to reflect her education. I gave her exactly what she wanted, with the caveat that we review her pay after ninety days.

Those three months came and went, and she came to see me in my office. Not a restaurant located within a hotel, you'll notice—our place of business, where business is discussed. She told me just to give her whatever I felt she was earning, and I had to give her a very firm no. I love this employee's husband, and I think he's a great guy. The fact, though, is his education is capped at a bachelor's degree.

This woman went past this, earning a bachelor's, a master's, and a PhD while also giving birth to five human beings and working throughout. Was that really only worth $3,000? If that were a man, he wouldn't be shy about demanding six figures more to reflect that.

I have personally been offered salary packages that I knew for certain were lower than my male counterparts' and told to take it or leave it. I have done both over time, depending on a multitude of other circumstances. If I *really* wanted the job, I would take the job and quickly make them realize my worth. To me, quickly is ninety days. I can then approach my boss and show them on their own P&Ls what I'm worth—and it's their turn to take it or leave it!

If they're not prepared to increase my salary, that's their lookout. They'll have cold, hard data before them, however, that shows that allowing me to walk away will significantly impact their bottom line. I will not say that I have always received the raise that I wanted. I can say that I have received that raise, or I have left.

What Next?

We are living in very interesting times right now. There is still a discrepancy between the world the business leaders of today are comfortable with and the world younger employees want.

One thing we all have to remember is when we're new to the world of business, we don't get to call the shots and change the whole culture of a company. It's like getting the "bad" shifts when you first start a new job—you have to earn the "good" ones!

Be the change you want to see in the world. Make people sit up and take notice of you by performing and showing them another way. Perhaps most important, show that women are just as capable of performing in the business world as men.

It offends people that I talk about the gender pay gap, but it really should offend them more that it exists.

> **Ultimately, women in the workplace work three times as hard as their male coworkers for two-thirds of their pay.**

That can't continue, and we all need to do our part to change that. It won't happen overnight, but if we all sit on our hands, it won't happen at all. That is simply not acceptable. All of us—men and women—owe it to ourselves and the people who we care about to put this right, one paycheck at a time.

Chapter Three

Image and Accountability

n my last chapter, I spoke at length about the difficulties I have faced in dealing with men in corporate America. Well, spoiler alert—that will continue throughout the pages of this book. It will no doubt carry on long after I have finished writing, too, unhappy as that makes me.

> Rome wasn't built in a day, and we can't break down decades of institutional sexism overnight.

There's a flip side to this, however, and I want to make one thing clear: women in positions of power are not always sunshine and rainbows to work with either. In fact, some of the biggest issues I've had in the workplace have involved other women— their expectations of me, their attitudes toward me, and their treatment of me. I gave a specific example when I mentioned the boss that attempted to use me as leverage for a preferential mortgage. In this chapter, I'm going to pull the curtain back a little further.

Setting the Table

There's an old proverb that "the road to Hell is paved with good intentions." An example of this was the Make Your Seat at the Table movement that arose a number of years ago.

This was an undertaking designed to assure that every major American corporation had at least one executive female voice in their boardroom. In theory, this would ensure that women stopped being overlooked in the corporate world and some very welcome diversity would make its way into a number of industries.

Can you see the problem here? We're talking *a seat* at the table. Seat, singular. I'm not a mathematician, but when we consider that women make up 50 percent of the population, those numbers still seem a little skewed to me. As you can probably imagine, competition became pretty fierce. Women would work hard—I'm going to call it here, harder than most men—to get this solitary seat at the table. Once they got there, these women would become extremely defensive about their position, fighting tooth and nail to hold onto it. That resulted in actions and attitudes that many people consider to be unhelpful or unwelcoming. There just wasn't room for multiple female executives or board members for the longest time.

Ironically, the one working environment I have ever been in with no cattiness was the Radio City Rockettes. There was a real sisterhood in the Rockettes, especially because being new is so grueling and overwhelming. We all knew that there was no room for emotion on the stage—we all had a job to do, and we were all pulling in one direction. Whatever happened, the show had to go ahead and we all had to be on our game. That didn't mean that nobody grated on your nerves. It just meant that you were responsible for taking yourself out of that environment.

I mention this because *how* women approached their positions of power has been an issue. In the past, when women reached the higher echelons of corporate America, they seemingly forgot everything that got them there and started to behave like their male colleagues. The suppressed became the suppressor, and they'd keep other women down and reinstate the glass ceiling they worked so hard to shatter. I know that I experienced that first hand, but as I've explained, I'm not the kind of person to go along with that!

Thankfully, this is really starting to change. What we have seen in the last several years is that people are less defensive. That doesn't just include women, but obviously we're still viewed with suspicion by some. Ultimately, however, people are prepared to make more seats for smart, hard-working women who can make a difference to a company. Finally, corporate America is becoming a meritocracy.

Personally, I consider merit to be key. Sometimes you'll see companies clearly filling in a check box. They need X amount of women and Y numbers of minorities in positions of power, so they'll bring in people who are least likely to rock the boat and will toe the existing line. These companies aren't trying to do what's right—they're trying to tick a box. Now, however, more and more women and minorities are achieving things because they have earned them and have great ideas.

Time Is Precious. Use it Wisely.

Life is all about picking your battles and choosing which hills you're prepared to die on. I've been reminded of this throughout my corporate life. I have a very strict philosophy when it comes to workplace roadblocks, and it's served me well.

> If you're running a race and it looks like you're never going to win it, change lanes. Do things your way, and get out of everybody else's slipstream.

There's a rat race in every industry. Sometimes it's friendly competition, and sometimes it's underhanded backstabbing. If you can sidestep all that and find your own path to success and happiness, you'll go a lot further. How do I know this? Because I didn't always practice what I preach! I'd like to say that I've always managed to avoid getting sucked into this nonsense, but that's just not the case.

You know the old saying, "Never wrestle with a pig. You'll both end up muddy, but the pig will enjoy it"? Well, just the other day I found myself wrestling with pigs on social media. I'm much better at avoiding these situations now than I was in my twenties, but it does happen—I'm human. If something is personal to me, I'll take it on.

It's not always about opinions and who is right and who is wrong. Sometimes it's about facts! If you present the facts and somebody else will not acknowledge them, there's nothing you can do about it. I realized this recently, when I was caught up in an argument with somebody who simply refused to accept the facts presented to them. Eventually, I had to accept that I was the fool in this situation. I do what I do, and that *doesn't* include interacting with online trolls. I mean, really, who has the time for that? If I take time out of my schedule to do so, that's on me.

It can be hard, though, because of the position I'm in. Ultimately, I am the boss of my company. Sometimes, when potentially harmful misinformation about the industry is being spread, it requires somebody with authority to step in, confront that, and get the truth out there. That's *all* I need to do though—get the correct information out and leave. Why should I spend time arguing with somebody who has built an unassailable opinion based on five minutes of internet research? I have spent years immersing myself in this world!

Sometimes, things take a turn for the personal too. People will say, "The CEO of JVZoo said X or Y." Well, everybody in this industry knows that *I* am the CEO of JVZoo, so they're essentially claiming, "Laura Casselman said X or Y." Most of the time, these things are snippets of a conversation that has been taken completely out of context! In those situations, I'll share a full transcript and leave it at that. I don't need to stay and argue—that's a waste of my time and energy and my board's money. I may mutter under my breath, but I remember that this is a keyboard cowboy, and I'm the CEO of JVZoo! There will always be a cycle of people in this world that just love to be contrary. If you want to be a Flat Earther, that's your lookout. Just don't talk about it on my time!

Wishy-washy people who waste my time don't tend to stick around long in my world. I have explained this before. It's not that I'm rude—I just don't have time for things that really don't matter when I'm at work. My team knows this. Is your child sick? I'm genuinely sorry to hear that. Take a seat, talk about it, and tell me if there's anything I can do to make this horrible situation more bearable. Is it raining outside? I hadn't noticed, and I don't much care.

I have a contractor that works for me, and we have a running joke. The first time we worked together, he spent five minutes talking about wine before he got started. I had to cut him off in the end and explain that he didn't know me and that this was a waste of my time. I don't care what wine he likes, and I don't have any inclination to discuss the wine that *I* like. I'll happily talk about wine with my mom over a cheeseboard or with my friends in a restaurant. In this situation, he wanted to work with my company, and I wanted to know why. Nothing else mattered.

Now, it's become an ongoing joke. He asks if I've had a good red recently, and I ask how many sales he's made! He's adamant that one day he'll get me to talk wine with him, but I just don't see it happening. He doesn't live near me—our conversations take place entirely over the phone, in the office, during my working day. If we ever have a business meeting in a restaurant, then, fine, that's a different ball game. At work though? That's just five minutes of my time that I'll never see again. I really don't have enough time to spare to start handing it out.

Success Breeds Contempt

In business, just like in life, there will always be people looking to contradict somebody more successful than them. Perhaps I should rephrase that, now that I think about it. There will always be people looking to contradict somebody *perceived* to be more successful.

Success is such a subjective term, and everybody's personal definition will be different. A lot of people don't want to be the CEO of a company. They don't want that level of responsibility or stress. They want to be able to walk away at the end of a working day and get on their fishing boat or spend time with their family, knowing that nobody will be calling their personal cell with business questions and emergencies. They're perfectly happy and bear no ill will toward anybody society would deem more successful. They have found what makes them happy and are living their best life. This is something I'll discuss in much greater detail in Chapter 4.

The internet has changed our definition of success too. Nowadays, everybody puts the highlight reel of their lives online, and others get jealous of this. The irony is, it's not even real half the time! People post doctored images that have been Photoshopped to remove wrinkles when we don't even know what they look like. Women sometimes message me and tell me how beautiful my Facebook photo is. My response is always the same—go through the *rest* of my photos! Sure my profile picture is a good one. That's why I chose it as my profile picture; I was putting my best foot forward! Scroll through, though, and you'll find plenty of shots with no makeup and my hair piled up while I'm on a boat in Jamaica. I may not look so good, but good grief, I was having fun!

That's the problem, though, as I see it.

> **As a society, we have all become so image conscious that we don't look beyond the superficial. It feels like being *seen* as doing something is more important than actually *doing it*.**

We have people paying to sit in private airplanes that they don't own, or haven't even hired for the day, so they can post a picture on social media and make it look like they took an exotic trip somewhere. They didn't go anywhere—they just spent $500 to have their photo taken on a plane. Their followers don't have to know that though. They just assume that this person has a glamorous jet-set lifestyle and react accordingly!

The world of Instagram influencers has also taken a turn. We now have people purchasing luxury goods, taking photos for their Instagram profiles, and acting like they were sent these things for free. They're hoping the companies will see this and *actually* start sending them free products, but why would they? They know they have a captive customer who is prepared to spend money on their brand! Image is such a strange thing, and I really wish we could all just focus on doing what we do best. If we channel our energies into that, we will build a positive image organically.

Reputation Matters

You know what's a whole lot more important than image? Reputation. I still need to portray myself a certain way at work if I want to achieve results. When I'm with friends or I'm in an informal setting, I'm chatty. I'm relaxed. During a seventeen-hour working day, however, I just don't have time for that. I'm direct, I'm to the point, and I want to understand what is happening and on what timescale. I'd like to claw at least some of my life back, and that's not going to happen if I fritter away hours on idle gossip about the weather and wine.

I've recently been pulling teeth while dealing with the executives of a major company. This business is much bigger than JVZoo, and the people I'm dealing with are all older white men. I think this is worth mentioning, given some of the treatment I've been receiving!

I have had to swallow a lot of pride when dealing with these people, because my job is to do the best I can for JVZoo. In fact, I've had to bring in male executives and ask them to take the lead on the call with this company, because the people I'm dealing with will not accept a woman in my position. My team understands that this happens—they laughed at first, because they knew it was killing me! We agreed on a strategy, though, and I act as an air traffic controller on our conference calls. Whenever there is a question from the other business, I assign somebody else on my team to talk them through the answer.

Sometimes, however, that just isn't possible. There have been a number of occasions that only I could speak up. Whenever I had the apparent audacity to do so, I was interrupted *every f'ing time.*

Pardon my French, but that never fails to grind my gears. When I was asked to explain the pain points I was experiencing, I managed to get twenty seconds into my explanation before I was cut off with, "I don't know who you are, young lady, but I did not get on this call to be berated."

Look, I'm from the South. I can make my voice as sweet as sugar when I need to! All the same, I wanted to slap myself for playing the game. That's what I did though. That's what I *have* to do, for the sake of doing business. Is it right? No. Is it fair? *Heck* no. That doesn't change the fact that I get labeled as a witch with a b almost immediately when I speak up to a male counterpart. What gives me the right to talk to people this way? they ask. Well, how about the fact that I just pushed a billion dollars through your system! These are questions that would be put to a male CEO, with all ears listening to his response, but to me, a female CEO, the question was really rhetorical, right? No need for me to actually open my pretty little mouth!

Another company we work with has provided nothing but headaches when it comes to their product. Despite this, their CEO is using my name to drive business to his platform. He is shouting from the rooftops that Laura Casselman of JVZoo trusts him and his product enough to utilize it. Naturally, this means that his potential customers are reaching out to me and asking if I really love this product as much as he says I do.

I have to set them straight and explain that I'm still attempting to integrate and I'll let them know the results, one way or another. Eventually, I had enough of this and told the CEO of this troublesome company exactly that. I asked him to stop using my name to shill his software until he'd managed to resolve the many and varied issues that JVZoo was still experiencing with it. His response was a patronizing—and wholly misplaced—"Laura, I have worked in technology for thirty-six years."

Well, in that case, I take it all back! Or, to be more accurate, I couldn't be less impressed. Unless you were working with NASA, nobody cares about technology thirty-six years ago. Wow, you were around for the first solar-powered calculator? Give me a break. Even *ten* years ago in technology is a very different landscape than now. I don't need your resume. I need your product to work as you advertise it.

His follow-up was that I wasn't taking any responsibility for the problems we were experiencing. I asked for an explanation about what we could be doing differently, and he had no idea. He just wanted me and JVZoo to shoulder some of the responsibility, although it was *his* broken API and *his* broken sandbox. Apparently, I should consider that perhaps my developers are not skilled enough to work around these deficiencies. He just had no idea how to speak to a female CEO and refused to admit that his company made mistakes.

This lack of accountability is something that never sits right with me. Remember the title of our last chapter? This is another example of how male CEOs do not see me as their equal. I'm the one who needs to reel in the call and build bridges. I'm the one who needs to put on my sweet voice and make him feel good about the deficiencies in his product. I can't be too direct and point out that our problems stem from their software. I can't state, "You guys gave me a broken API." It has to be, "Now, where do we think this broken API came from?"

There's another thing to remember about workplace reputations, too, especially for women. They can take a long time to build and can be seriously damaged with one careless or vindictive remark. More than once I've had subordinates and colleagues—

male and female—make comments along the lines of, "Huh, no prizes for guessing what *she* did to get that position."

I remember once being sat at a corporate dinner table with my then CEO to my left and my direct competitor straight in front of me. She sat down, looked me square in the eye, and said, "So, what's it like sleeping with the CEO to get your job?"

She knew that I hadn't so much as *flirted* with him, and she knew exactly what she was doing. All the senior figures of the company were there, and she was stirring the pot with rumor and innuendo in an attempt at flustering me. Sadly, it worked. A number of people started to give me the side-eye, clearly wondering if there was any truth to her statement, and I completely lost my appetite.

It was so uncomfortable for all concerned—including the CEO in question. He was married and felt that he had to move seats. He had positioned himself next to me because I was the top-performing person in the company, and this dinner was supposed to be celebrating my workplace results. Now, suddenly, I was persona non grata—all because of a vindictive and jealous comment. Would that have happened to a male team member? I'll let you decide for yourself.

I've also had men flat out tell me they'd be so much better at my job than me. I'm always willing to give them a chance to prove that—I ask them what they know about the role. They never seem able to answer that. I guess they're just born better in their minds!

To this day, even as a CEO, I still have people make rude comments to and about me. It always makes me laugh when a male colleague calls me. He'll say that he's seen something posted online, and while he knows that I can handle it myself, he's ready and willing to step in and shut it down if I want him to! I think that's great, but if I ask somebody else to help out, it looks like I can't handle it. Guess what? I can! That's what happens when you spend your life battling these kinds of idiots.

What's in a Name?

I remember a story that went viral on Twitter a while ago. It was written up as articles all over the web, so you'll be able to find it with a little Googling. Two colleagues, Martin Schneider and Nicole Hallberg, were supposed equals but were achieving very different results in their jobs. Their boss was getting frustrated because Martin was performing so much higher with clients than Nicole. Clients seemed to hang on his every word but kept kicking back and growing frustrated with Nicole, saying that she took too long to service their requests.

Things changed when Martin emailed a client that he had a great relationship with and got a really angry, uncharacteristic response. He thought it was a little odd and realized that he had accidentally attached Nicole's email signature. They did an experiment and pretended to be each other for a week. They worked and communicated in the same way they always did, but as far as the clients were concerned, they were different genders. Can you guess how this story ends?

Martin realized that Nicole had to explain herself three times and that people were constantly rude and disrespectful to her. Nicole, meanwhile, was stunned that she only had to say things once and clients called it the greatest idea they'd ever heard. It's crazy.

At the time of writing, there is a whole lot of controversy surrounding a Gillette commercial about toxic masculinity. Even if the chatter has died down by the time you read this, run a search on YouTube—it's bound to be around there still. Now, speaking for myself, I don't care if people support that commercial or don't.

That's their lookout. Speaking as a woman in corporate America, however, the opening scene made my skin crawl.

The image is of a woman speaking in the boardroom, and a man places his hands on her shoulders and interrupts with, "I think what she's trying to say is . . ." I have been in that position so many times. I *know* what I'm trying to say. I was in the process of saying it before you stepped in. Let me speak for myself, and don't chastise me by placing your hands on my shoulder. I'm not your daughter. If you see that kind of behavior, step up and put a stop to it!

This is why I think it's so important that everybody speaks out when they see a woman being mistreated in the workplace—regardless of whether you're male or female. Stand up and point out these things. Don't let people interrupt women in the boardroom. Men get to talk for hours, but most women are cut off after thirty seconds. If there's a female executive in the room, don't let a man demand that she takes notes. Don't single out the sole female to ask about the parking facilities or the catering. Why would they know? They're in the room to do business, just like everybody else.

These steps may not seem like much, but they're so pivotal. They could be the difference between a skilled, smart, and talented woman receiving the recognition she deserves and turning around the fortunes of an ailing company, or eventually growing tired of the constant fight and walking away. Nobody wins in the latter situation, so why would anybody think it's appropriate? Everybody with a seat at that table has earned it, and especially if it's a woman, they will have worked incredibly hard for it! That effort demands recognition, and that woman deserves to be treated with respect.

Chapter Four

Be Responsible for Your Own Dang Happiness!

Happiness is a strange thing. It's so important to all of us, and yet it's something that so many people neglect. Whether you're thinking about your personal or professional life, you've got to take responsibility for your own happiness. Expecting somebody to do it for you is akin to relinquishing control of your own life.

Let's look at happiness at work in the first instance. Let's be blunt—we spend more time at work than anything else. If we're miserable in our career, it will always bleed into our personal lives. When did you last meet a happy-go-lucky individual that admitted their job made them want to jump off a bridge?

I derive my happiness from experiencing contentment in the work I'm doing. Now, the great thing about that is that it's a seriously broad church. Contentment varies from person to person, and it all starts with *why* you work. Do you need to feel a purpose in your work, or are you just earning a paycheck? There is no right or wrong answer here, and either is fine. What's important is that *you* build your working life around *your* needs. That's not anybody else's job.

Personally, I need to feel a purpose at work. It's never been solely about the remuneration package for me; I need to feel that I'm helping somebody or making a difference. I have never been able to settle for being just another cog in the wheel. I have always set goals, ever since I was little. I take a great deal of pride in setting a goal and then accomplishing it, and pride plays a major role in my personal happiness.

For the longest time, this sense of pride was related to sales. My first entrepreneurial experiences came from selling Girl Scout cookies, and I loved that. Maybe more importantly, I loved selling the *most* Girl Scout cookies of anybody in my troop! That was a form of winning for me, and I like to win.

I carried this experience over to corporate America when I moved into this world. I naturally gravitated toward sales jobs because that's what I knew I enjoyed. As time went on, however, I started to feel that I needed *more*. I wanted to start impacting people's lives and livelihoods for the better. That's perfectly natural. We all evolve as time goes on, and I'm no exception. I occasionally feel as though I digress on my path, but it's all part of the same journey!

Personal journeys are also why some people work just for a paycheck, though, and I completely respect that. Personal journeys, like everything in this world, have to be paid for. If you're looking to earn money to finance what really matters to you, then cool. You just have to ask yourself what's enough to *fulfill* you while you're earning that paycheck. If you walk away from your shift with a sense of contentment and then get real joy from a personal passion project, then congratulations. You have unlocked the key to personal happiness!

Achieving Trumps Obtaining

Now, at the risk of sounding like I'm yelling at kids to get off my lawn, I've noticed a shift toward in-workplace mentality in recent years. As the new wave of younger generations joins the ranks of us working stiffs, it's becoming apparent that many younger people have unrealistic expectations of changing the world immediately.

Look, I'm not belittling the future leaders of our planet here. I'm not saying that there isn't a twenty-year-old out there capable of changing the world. Look at Mark Zuckerberg. He changed the way the whole world communicates while he was still in college. What I *am* saying, however, is that there are maybe five or ten people in every generation who will have that large of an impact. When we compare that to the sheer number of people entering the workplace, those odds aren't great!

I would never, *ever* discourage a young person from aiming high. Personally, I don't understand people who don't.

> **It takes the same amount of effort to think big as it does to think small, after all.**

However, it takes action for things to change. It's hard to make that kind of impact. As a result, I consider it a mistake for younger generations to think they're going to change the world in their first job.

My advice would be to change one person's world at a time. Make one person's day a little better—there will always be that trickle-down effect. We see it in Coca-Cola commercials. Somebody shares a cola with a friend, who smiles at an old lady, who pets a dog, who puts a smile on a child's face, who makes a new friend in the playground . . . These little things *do* have a butterfly effect. Expecting to change the world at large with your first job is a little unrealistic though.

First, you have to ask yourself an important question. Apart from the names of all the different Pokémon, what does anybody *really* know at the age of twenty? I sometimes compare my twenty-year-old self, bless her heart, to the woman I am today. There are things about that younger Laura that I miss, but I know a whole lot more about how the world works now!

I've been speaking pretty broadly about young people in the workplace so far, so I'd like to make something clear: I don't consider all Gen Z to be a hive mind. In fact, I'd say that the new generation could be split almost in half. I see a lot of young people with the same entrepreneurial spirit that I had at their age. They're bursting with ideas, and they're prepared to roll up their sleeves and make things happen. I understand these kids and will go out of my way to do anything I can to help, advise, and nurture them on their journey.

Unfortunately, they only amount to around 50 percent of Generation Z. Maybe even a little less. Some of these kids don't want to put in the effort and consider it unfair that they have to work for their paycheck. They think they deserve the same wage on their first day as a coworker with sixteen years of experience and knowledge. They claim it's not fair that they're assigned the scrub shifts on evenings and weekends when they want to be out with their friends.

Can you guess what I think about that attitude? That's right. It's BS. Pay your dues. None of us are owed a darn thing when we're born. Everything is earned, and nothing should be handed to us (except love, and that should come free of charge!). The only way we'll ever get where we want to be is by putting in the work. There is a sense of accomplishment that comes from working for something that simply can't be matched by having it handed over on a silver platter.

I don't care if somebody considers that attitude to be unfair. Guess what, kids—life isn't fair. If your parents told you that it was, they lied to you. The moon isn't made of cheese either, in case you were wondering.

> **Life isn't fair—but then it isn't *unfair* either. Life is indifferent, because the world doesn't revolve around any single one of us.**

The sooner we all accept and understand this, the happier we'll all be.

Learn Happiness from Hardship

I sometimes think that adversity and difficulty are pivotal to happiness. I understand that sounds a little oxymoronic, but it's true. Until we have been tested—mentally, physically, and emotionally—we never really know *what* we're capable of when the going gets tough. Obviously none of us wants to be sick or to be impacted negatively. Once we have overcome struggle and challenges, though, we can start to really take control of our own lives.

One way to overcome adversity is to always have a goal. I mentioned earlier that I have been goal oriented for longer than I can remember. It was also very important to me to always have a plan A, B, C, and D. Life is rarely a straight line, and we will be thrown regular curveballs. Pardon my mixing of sporting metaphors, but this means that we have to roll with these punches and adapt where necessary.

These days, things are a little different. I have experienced enough in my life that I'm confident in my ability to pivot when I need to. This means that I'm less concerned with planning things to the *n*th degree. I'll always have ideas in the back of my head—that's just my nature. I just don't sit down and plan them like I used to. When I was younger, I'd all but have charts drawn up that devised every possible twist and turn a scenario could take.

Don't get me wrong, though—I'm not a masochist that enjoys struggle! Struggle sucks. If life came with an opt-out tick box that meant we could enjoy a year of plain sailing with no adversity, we'd all tick it every time. That doesn't mean that we don't learn from our hardships though. What seems like the worst experience in our lives during the moment can often end up being hugely important to our personal development. These days, I look back and almost laugh at what I once considered to be huge personal battles. I thought *that* was hard? Every one of those difficult times taught me a sense of perspective. They provide me with assurance that, whatever happens, problematic moments always pass.

I recently had to lay off a new hire, and I knew it was her first time being let go from anywhere. I felt for her so much because I remember what that feels like. It feels like a rejection of you as a human, which really isn't the case! I sat down with her and made sure she knew she hadn't done anything wrong, and her performance had been spot-on. It was just one of those situations that comes up in business. I felt so awful, though, even though I knew she had learned a whole lot and would be even better in her next job.

She called me two days later to let me know she had already started a new job. She explained that she *had* learned a lot from her coworkers and me, and she was just hurt because she loved her job working with me. I'm pretty sure she'd be absolutely fine if I reached out to her now. She went through a trial, and she came out the other side of it with a new life experience. She'll no doubt use that experience in the future to console a friend when the same thing happens to them.

Another reason struggle is so important is that it helps us learn what *doesn't* work for us. If we're going to be happy people, we need to eliminate negative experiences and influences from our lives where applicable. We need to stop following patterns that don't bring us joy. Instead, we need to focus on the things we *want* to be doing in our life.

That doesn't have to be anything grand and earth-shattering either. It could be getting out of bed an hour earlier so you can fit more into your day. It could be working out every day. It could be carving out fifteen minutes every day to read. It could be doing something that makes life easier for your boss or your customers. Identify those checkboxes. Even if you don't experience immediate gratification while filling them, you'll be able to look back later and feel like a bad*ss! Now is the time to bask in the glow of your accomplishments.

Sometimes, we just need to push through in the short term to feel better in the end. After a long, exhausting day, it's hugely tempting to pick up fast food rather than prepare a healthy meal from scratch. We're always glad if we resist the easy option, though, as we feel so much better for it afterward.

Find Your Happy

So many people don't know what makes them happy and how to sustain and prioritize that. I'm sure that's an awful way to live. Maybe that's why there is so much misery and hate in the world.

Look at what's happening in the world every time we turn on the news. Mass shootings, stabbing sprees, people throwing acid over each other . . . What *causes* these things? It sure isn't happiness. Happy people just don't do those things.

> **Happy people don't hurt others.**

We need to focus on what brings us joy as individuals—not what will save the world. That's important, too, but it's not something we can achieve in a day. We need to know what makes *us* happy.

When I'm in a funk, I sit down and look at what has changed in my life. Oftentimes, it's that I'm working so many hours that I haven't been exercising every day. That is a huge deal for me. I know that I need to exercise to feel good in my own skin, and I know that I need to feel good in my own skin to be happy.

Sometimes, I realize that I have been so consumed with work that I haven't reached out to my friends in the longest time. I love my job, but I still need that balance, so I take the necessary action. Most problems always seem smaller when you're sharing them with good company over dinner and a bottle of wine.

Another thing I miss is reading. I used to read three books a week, as I love taking in new knowledge and enjoying a darn good story. I don't currently have as much time for that, but I make sure I still have some time to read. I can fit in a book every week or two. That's enough to make me happy.

Ultimately, I don't need to purchase anything to make me happy either. It doesn't cost me a thing to tie my shoes and go for a run outside my house. I can go to the library and get a good book. Spending time with my family and being a good mom, daughter, sibling, and friend—those are all free, they matter to me, and they contribute heavily to my happiness.

It seems to me that most children in the modern world have no idea how to be happy, and that breaks my heart. Parents don't know how to help their kids either, because they tend to be unhappy adults. I saw so many dance moms trying to live vicariously through their children while I worked on the stage that I know I'll never imitate *that* behavior.

I will always be more concerned with helping my daughter find happiness than her grade on a trigonometry test or what role she takes in the school play. Being a happy, self-sufficient, good human being is far more important to me than any report card or accolade.

I talk to a relative of mine about this a lot, as her child currently isn't involved in any kind of team sports or group activity. Maybe he doesn't like sports. That's fine—they're not for everybody. There are always other options, though, including the arts—a subject that's obviously close to my heart. Being part of a group activity as a kid teaches us so many lessons. Even if that lesson is just, "I don't like group activities!"

I still maintain that it's important. It's possible that a kid will play baseball and decide they don't enjoy it. What they might find, however, is that they love the adrenaline rush of *winning*. Equally, that same kid may hate competing but love the community spirit that comes from being part of a team.

That can't be taught any other way than through trial and error. Let your kids learn. My parents made me have piano lessons as a kid, and I hated it. I absolutely loathed it! However, it did teach me that I loved *music*. That played a role in leading me to a career on the stage, and I adored every moment of that.

My time onstage also taught me a lot about what makes me happy. I learned about how much I like to win—whether that's nailing a dance routine in a rehearsal room or wowing the casting director at an audition. That world also taught me a lot about empathy. People are regularly belittled and berated in rehearsals, and even auditions. It wasn't unheard of for me to take the train home in tears, having had strips torn off me and still not getting a job. After a while it became like water off a duck's back, but the early stages were tough.

Ultimately, though, I stuck at it. I kept my discipline, which is essential for a dancer. I often say that dancers are not just athletes—they're among the hardest-working athletes in the world. The sense of self-discipline and tunnel vision you need as a professional dancer is not teachable. Why would I put myself through the rejection, the hard training, the injuries, and the emotional turmoil? Because it made me happy, and happiness is *always* worth fighting for.

Easy Come, Easy Go

Long-term happiness is something that's very important to me. Unfortunately, it appears to be a lost art in the twenty-first century and the age of social media. It seems to me that everybody is looking for a quick fix of joy, or an adrenaline shot of happiness. There seems to be an attitude of, "I told that person their opinion was wrong on the internet and called them a disgusting human being. I am one of life's winners now—I've achieved something."

You know the trouble with that? That happiness is fleeting—if you can even call it happiness. Does being a keyboard cowboy and attacking other people online *really* bring you contentment? If so,

I'd hate to live your life. That's just a crapshoot. You're reliant on other people constantly feeding you with things to criticize, and upon gaining the response you want afterward. There are far more constructive ways to spend your time—starting with figuring out what actually makes you happy.

I talked about the social media phenomenon in the previous chapter, but it's something that endlessly fascinates me. Especially Instagram, that's a great one for understanding what makes some people tick. I occasionally flick through Instagram profiles of people and marvel at their amazing photos. They have these fantastic shots from where they're traveling, looking amazing without a hair out of place, and I wonder why I can't take such perfect photos. Then I remember it's because when I'm traveling, I'm more concerned with living in the moment! I would rather do that and talk about the experience with my friends afterward, than spend hours of every day fussing and worrying about getting the perfect photo to project a certain image.

There's a song called "Photograph" by the folk singer Richard Julian where he sings about preferring memories to photographs. That has always stuck with me. When I'm old and gray, it will be my memories that give me comfort. I'll be able to think back on the amazing times I had and the experiences that stayed with me forever. I wouldn't be able to say the same thing if I did and saw nothing in a new country because I wasted an entire day on hair, makeup, and picking out the ideal pose and filter for my photo on Insta.

I think social media also creates a huge disconnect in our relationship with material things. Some people browse social media and get so hung up on what they don't have. People think that if they had enough money to buy X or look like Y, they'd be happy. It doesn't work that way. In most circumstances, you'll end up in debt to finance what you wanted, which will just cause stress. In others, you'll get what you thought was missing from your life . . . and then what?

You'll have a moment of happiness. It may even be an extended moment. Unfortunately, though, it *will* pass. Human beings are not jigsaw puzzles. We're not just missing one piece that will make us whole. Happiness comes from within us, not from stuff. Possessions just provide fleeting moments of contentment, and then you'll be looking for the next short-term fix.

Here's an example: right now, there is a house on the market that I want. And let me make something clear—I *want* this house! It's in the right location, and it already looks perfect. I wouldn't have to change a thing about it. On paper, living in that house would make me happy.

Unfortunately, I also consider the asking price too high for me to pay right now, for multiple reasons. Sure, I could empty a substantial amount of my savings, cut the realtor a check for a deposit, and buy the house. I'm pretty sure I would then feel like a queen for a few months while I settled in and hosted amazing cocktail parties for my friends.

That impact wears off though. It's like an artificial high before cold, hard reality sets in. I would have to replenish the money I had extracted from my savings in order to feel secure and comfortable in myself. I would also be on the hook for huge monthly payments. Even leaving the mortgage aside, heating, cooling, and insuring a house of that size doesn't come cheap.

That would just cause me more stress in the longer term. I'm not a lottery winner or a billionaire. I'm pretty much stretched to breaking point when it comes to my time as it is. I literally *can't* work more hours to increase my income. If anything, I'd like to start clawing some of my life back and working fewer hours a week. I'd just be creating a rod for my own back for the sake of short-term happiness, so the time isn't right.

It's a shame though. I really do love that house! (sigh)

Strike a Balance

In 2009, I was diagnosed with a pituitary tumor. That had a *major* impact on my personal and professional lives for around three years. At the time, those were the worst times of my life. The medication I was on would have me getting up from my desk every few hours to puke my brains out. Then I'd go back to work as though nothing happened. It was a real mental battle. That was nothing compared to what was to come, though.

A few years ago, my father got sick, so sick that his whole life changed. That was so hard for me. My own health problems? I could deal with those. I *did* deal with those. Watching my dad struggle was different, though, and in many respects, it was worse. This wasn't my battle to fight, and there was literally nothing I could do to fix it. None of us enjoy watching people we love experience hurt or struggle. We want those burdens to come to us so *we* can carry them on our own shoulders. Unfortunately, life doesn't work that way.

I bring this up because when we don't know what's coming next, achieving balance in our lives can be challenging. We all need to find that sweet spot between living for the moment and not making decisions that will enslave our future selves. I am still learning this myself.

Take saving as an example. As I have already said, I'm reluctant to diminish my savings to buy this dream house. I'm a type A—I can't help but think about my retirement, as I want to retain control over my entire life, including my twilight years. I know exactly how much money I need in my retirement fund to feel comfortable.

However, I also keep a vacation account so I can get out there and see the world and do cool stuff. I work hard *right now* (including on my vacations, such is the nature of my role!), and I want to enjoy the moment. I don't want to put my entire life on hold while I'm young in order to have money when I retire.

I think I have managed to find my balance, but everybody places their line in a different place. Some people live at extreme ends of the line though. Some people are adamant that they're going to live exclusively in the moment and not think about what they'll do when they're seventy and still need to work like a horse every day just to pay their bills. Others are so concerned with what the future holds that they hoard every cent they earn, waiting for a rainy day and forgetting to enjoy today.

My parents are a slight example of the latter. I spent the last six years or so telling them they should spend some of the savings they had accrued on life experiences, while they were still young enough to enjoy them. They don't owe my sister and me a thing. We are adults that have moved out of the house. There is no need to leave us a dime—we can take care of ourselves.

My parents wouldn't spend that money though. They kept holding onto it for that fabled rainy day. What if something happened to my sister or me? What if we needed that money? Well, we didn't—but as I mentioned, my dad got very sick. He has recovered, thank goodness, but he's not the same person he was.

As I write this, I'm preparing to take my parents on their first-ever international vacation. We're off to Europe to see the Northern Lights. It's exciting, and I'm looking forward to it, but it's still tinged with a little sadness and regret. A year ago, my dad was as healthy as an ox. He would have relished and enjoyed every minute of this trip. I'm sure he still will, but now he has to take what seems like three gallons of medication. We now need to monitor his compression on the airplane and make sure he gets up and walks around enough. We need to be careful about what he eats, as there is now a long list of foods he can't have.

He'll still have a good time. It's just a shame he didn't have this experience before we had to think about this stuff. This is what I mean by striking a balance. If you wait too long for a rainy day, you may find yourself trapped in an unexpected storm.

Laugh in the Face of Fear

Some people let fear stand in the way of their happiness. Whether that's fear of failure, ridicule, rejection, or anything else. I'll be honest—that's not something I can speak on with any real authority. Fear, typically, isn't something I experience a lot. I just never have.

I think that comes from having an amazing childhood, where I had nothing to fear. Anything I was scared of as a kid was self-in-flicted, like when I watched the movie *Poltergeist* and ended up with a lifelong phobia of clowns! Alternatively, maybe it's my background on the stage. If you're going to make a living in the creative world, you learn a *lot* about rejection and how not to fear it!

Take Misty Copeland as an example. Misty is the principal ballerina at the American Ballet Theater. If you don't follow ballet, that's a big deal—it's the dancer's equivalent of playing starting quarterback in the Super Bowl. These days, Misty is being signed up for endorsements left, right, and center. She likely has been rejected thousands of times in the past, though, purely because an athletic build was not acceptable in ballet until recently.

As an adult, fear is an interesting feeling for me. It's something that I often don't recognize. I need to take a step back and say, "Oh yeah, I'm scared right now." I like to sit with that for a moment, almost trying it on for size. I'll never let fear stand in my way of doing something though. At least not in the workplace. Obviously I have the same healthy fear instincts as everybody else. I have that gut reaction that tells me walking alone down a dark alley at night isn't a smart idea!

Overall, though, I see fear as more of a warning than a guiding influence in my life. More often, I'm excited to see what's going to happen. I like to win, which means that I'll never back down from a challenge. *That's* where I find my happiness. Once you learn how to trigger your own happiness, you'll find that everything clicks into place.

Commit to figuring out what makes you happy. It may take a while, but it *will* happen. In the meantime, also pay attention to what makes you *un*happy. There may be a kernel of joy buried in there somewhere that you haven't noticed. There's an inner child in all of us that hates baseball but loves to win.

Try anything and everything, and see what sticks. Sign up, and stick to it. Don't quit—see out a season, at the very least. And most importantly of all, don't wait for somebody else to find your happiness for you. That's a cop-out. Happiness is not going to fall into your lap, and you can't wait until life isn't hard anymore to decide to be happy (#nightbirde). You need to get off your booty and care enough about yourself to make it happen. You'll change your life if you do.

Chapter Five

Giving an *F*

We talked a lot about happiness in the last chapter and how important it is. I sincerely hope you've taken a moment to think about what makes *you* happy and what you can do to bring more joy into your life.

So many people don't know what makes them happy, as we discussed. One of the biggest impacts of this is that people care *way* too much about things that don't matter. Care about the stuff that matters to you, and stop giving an "*F*" about everything else. You gain nothing from it, and you're just bringing unnecessary strain and misery into your life.

Now, don't get this twisted. I'm not a sociopath that ignores anything in my life that isn't sunshine and rainbows. I *wish* that was the case, but it's simply not true. There are a whole lot of things in my life that make me deeply unhappy, but I still care about them.

Case in point—think back to the last chapter. I discussed how my dad was sick, and that was not easy for me. If there is one thing in the world that I care about above all else, it's my family. They come first, second, and third in my list of priorities. My family took care of me when I needed them, and now it's my turn to return that favor in whatever ways I can.

I don't grit my teeth, sigh heavily, and begrudgingly take care of my family because I feel a social obligation. I don't do it against my will, because I'm worried that other people will judge me harshly if I don't. I make my family a priority because they *matter*. They are my circle, and they are my happiness. I had to work on myself to understand that. I had to dig deep into my mind, body, and spirit and acknowledge that the health and well-being of my family matter to me.

Having said that, there are other things I care about too—things that would be stupid to many people. Here's the thing: they probably *are* stupid. I don't give an F though. They bring me joy, and that's enough for me.

Let's take shoes as an example. I like nice shoes, and I'm not going to apologize for that. I'm not saying shoes are more important than people, or that I could watch the world burn as long as I'm wearing a stylish pair of Christian Louboutin heels. In the grand scheme of things, shoes are not going to change my life.

Having said that, if I pick up a new pair of shoes that bring me joy, that makes me a happier human being, and that, in turn, makes me a better person. I'm more pleasant to be around, I feel more relaxed, and you know what? They look good too!

Success Matters

Take a look at what's important to you, and give an F about achieving or preserving it. When you care about something, you're much more likely to focus your energy on getting what you want. Most people say that success is important to them and they care about that. Great. Now you have to stop and think, though—what defines success for you?

I'm going to say that again, with a particular emphasis. What defines success for *you*? Not your friends. Not your coworkers. Not the prom king and queen that you're still measuring yourself against, years removed from high school. It's what *you* consider to be success that matters.

Some people don't need acclaim from their industry peers to feel successful. Somebody may build a website with the specific aim of helping a small, select group of people and achieve that aim. If that applies to you, and you're helping your target audience, give yourself a pat on the back. You are achieving success in what matters to you.

For some people, success means a job title. I totally get that. In fact, I felt the same way for the longest time. For other people, having a certain amount of money in the bank defines success. That's understandable too. Life in the twenty-first century is expensive and unpredictable.

As I touched upon in my last chapter, I don't feel safe and secure unless my savings account is at what I deem to be an acceptable level. Money is important to me, and I'd be lying if I said it wasn't. I'd give away everything I own and live in a cardboard box if it meant my family was taken care of, but I *definitely* care about financial security. This means that I focus a lot of my time and effort on maintaining that level of economic stability.

If your definition of success *doesn't* revolve around a paycheck, however, why give an *F* if somebody makes more money than you? It's easy to assume that money makes everybody happy, but do you really know the ins and outs of that person's affairs?

For all you know, they may take home a bigger salary but lose the vast majority of it to an overpriced mortgage on a house they can't sell. They may have a loved one that's seriously sick and spend almost every cent they earn on medical bills. Shoot, they may be *so* focused on their paycheck that they're constantly seething that somebody else earns more than them. That's not a happy and healthy way to be.

Just because somebody makes more money than you, it doesn't necessarily make them happier. Don't be jealous. Don't covet the fact they have a bigger house and a boat. That's their business, and it's not for you to give an *F* about. There will *always* be somebody in the world who has more material wealth than you. Constantly comparing yourself to others is a miserable way to live.

Again, I'm not saying not to care about *anything*. Pathological apathy won't get you anywhere. I'm saying do a little work on yourself, work out what matters to you, and care about *that*. Everything else is just white noise that distracts you from getting where you want to be.

The Green-Eyed Monster

I'm going to return to one of my favorite subjects now—social media. I genuinely feel that *so* many people would be happier if social media didn't exist.

I should probably clarify something here, though, before we go any further. I am not *against* social media, and I don't think that it should be abolished. I'm the CEO of a tech company—that would be like a turkey voting for Christmas! Social media itself is a neutral construct, neither good nor evil. What I am against is the way people *use* social media. So many people use their Instagram profiles to construct the narrative of a fake life, and so many people waste their energy on jealousy and resentment about that.

The world was easier when we could see people's faces and hear their voices. Now all we see are photographs that have been filtered to the point that they do not represent a moment in time. I'll refer you back to a previous example from Chapter 3. You may see a photo of a friend looking amazing with perfect hair and makeup, standing aboard a private plane. That could make you feel like you can't keep up. This person is living the dream, while you're stuck in a cubicle and worrying about whether your car will start tomorrow.

What you *won't* see is how this person maxed out their credit card renting that plane for an hour, just for this photo. How they spent weeks practicing hair and makeup when they could have been living their life, just to nail that photo. How their effortless pose and smile, which looked like a well-timed moment of contentment, was the hundredth photo taken because none of the others were perfect.

Are you really envious of somebody who cares *that* much about what other people think? Well, I'll admit, I am a little—I wish I had that kind of time on my hands! The point stands though. You're wasting your time and energy caring about something that *is not real*. Do you also get bent out of shape over the fact that Superman can fly and you can't?

You can acknowledge that something like this is visually pleasing. You can even throw this person the heart on Instagram that they so clearly live for! Just don't waste your life giving an *F* about the actions of other people and feeling that they are setting a competitive standard you can't live up to.

Let's be clear though. I do *understand* the mentality of envy. I went through a phase in my life when I was almost perennially envious, and I had to work on myself to get over it. Green is not my color, and I really knew that I didn't want to be that person.

I was envious of people who had better jobs than me. At that point, I wasn't practicing what I now preach. I considered anybody with a grander job title and a bigger paycheck to have a better job. I was living two lives at that point too. I had started working in corporate America, and I was still dancing professionally.

Instead of stopping to think that I was blessed to have two opportunities to achieve great things, I saw it as two opportunities to covet what other people had! On the one hand, I would look at somebody who was promoted to regional manager, while I was still a general manager. "How did *she* get that job? I am smarter than her. I should have gotten it." On the other hand, I'd see a fellow dancer get a job at Cirque du Soleil. "That should have been me! I am more talented than her!"

Of course, while I was in that mindset, I wasn't looking at the bigger picture. I had a foot on two wildly disparate ladders—nobody else could say that. I may have been one rung below each of these people on both ladders, but I was *on* both ladders. Nobody else could say that. If one of these ladders toppled over, I could hop onto the other without losing everything I had worked for.

That wasn't how I saw things at the time though. I wanted what these people had. I wanted it *all*. I wasn't cheering them on and enjoying their success, which is what I should have been doing. The right response was to congratulate them on busting their butts and achieving what they set out to do through hard work, determination, and dedication. Instead, I was, well, there's no point in mincing words here—I was being a *witch with a b*.

There's one problem with that—I'm not a witch with a b. I want everybody to succeed and find their happiness. That was a real wake-up for me and made me realize that I wasn't the person I wanted to be. That was nobody's fault but my own, and I was the only person who could fix the problem. I started to think about my own life and what I was good at doing. Once I knew that, I knew what I should care about. That also taught me how to be my own cheerleader.

I didn't need anybody else to tell me I was doing well. What mattered was that *I* felt happy and confident in what I was achieving. I was jealous because I wasn't focusing on what I needed; I was comparing myself to somebody else who was not living my path. That was when I reeled it back in and started cheering other people on.

> **As the writer Harold Coffin says, "Envy is the art of counting the other fellow's blessings instead of your own."**

Of course, I still experience the occasional pang of envy. I'm human! I have a very famous friend that I danced with in the Rockettes, and she now has a really coveted position on television. This means that I sometimes switch on my TV and see her on the red carpet with George Clooney or whoever.

Am I jealous of her in that moment? Heck yeah—in the best possible way! I'll often send her a message expressing that sentiment. I know how hard she worked for that opportunity, though, and I could not be more thrilled for her. That's a huge moment in her career, and it hasn't arisen by accident. Sure, I'd love to go and stand next to George Clooney, at least for a moment or two. I'd share the heck out of *that* on social media and give zero *F*s about any accusations of hypocrisy!

In the grand scheme of things, though, I don't really give an *F* about George Clooney's world. I don't care who designed his tuxedo or what he ate for breakfast that morning. I'd probably have a more interesting conversation with his wife, Amal, about her human rights work.

Again, would I like to go stand *next to* George Clooney for a minute or two? Yes. Am I prepared to put in the years of work and sacrifice that would grant me that opportunity? Nope! It would be a cool experience, but you've got to put the work in to earn that. I'm not prepared to do so, so I have no right to be jealous. What I do have a right to, and what I'm incredibly happy doing, is cheering my former Rockette sister on as all her continued hard work pays off. You go, Keltie Knight!

Be Your Own Cheer Squad

I think it's human nature to seek acknowledgment when you find your path. I certainly felt that when I started to go about things the right way, other people should have noticed that, or should they have?

They shouldn't. It's your journey, not theirs. Part of growth is experiencing new emotions and understanding the appropriate way to process them. We really need to be spending our entire lives checking ourselves and looking at our reactions.

I remember watching my friends move from 0 to 60 in their careers and acknowledging them the whole way. They weren't necessarily changing the world at that point, but I knew that they were on their way. Eventually, they got to where they deserve to be, and I felt a little hurt that they were not acknowledging my support and returning it to me.

This wasn't because they were ignoring me, though, or because they were ignorant. They were just *busy* kicking booty and taking names. If they stopped to take a bow every step of the way, they wouldn't have achieved as much as they did. Equally, when I started to climb the ladder, I felt as though I wasn't being seen.

I had to call myself out on that, stop caring so much about being acknowledged, and focus on what mattered to me.

Once I realized this, I had a conversation with one of my friends. I explained that I felt she hadn't seen me or cheered me along the way. She told me that she had seen *everything*. She wasn't disregarding my achievements, or disrespecting me. She just had her own ladder to climb and didn't have time to keep patting me on the head. She was still walking her own path.

We can laugh about this now. She always makes sure she checks in to say, "I see you. Don't be mad at me!" and I know she's kidding and just wants to make sure I don't feel neglected. Ultimately, though, I realized that I'm my *own* cheerleader.

Self-encouragement is an inside job.

I don't need a standing ovation or a medal for doing what I do (although I'll accept a pair of Jimmy Choos if anybody is offering).

My friends mean the world to me, but when they're busy busting their own tails on the other side of the world, a text message saying, "You go, girl!" isn't the end-all be-all of my happiness. I do what I do because it matters to me and because I care about it. A lot of what I value revolves around how I behave, what I contribute to the world, and what I get in return. If I'm not causing a scene while I'm achieving something, then I'm just efficiently getting on with my job. That's something I learned as a dancer, and I think all athletes have the same approach. It's about taking something hugely difficult and making it look easy.

Take the Olympics as an example. Watching on TV, throwing a javelin doesn't look so hard. Do I think that I could pick one up and break a world record though? I'm guessing that's a no. These competitors have dedicated their lives to training, practicing, and mastering their technique. That's what people who do a great job do. They make something hard look simple and effortless.

That applies to everything in life, right down to walking into a store and buying a new cell phone. You could walk into a store having cleared your schedule for an hour and walk out five minutes later with a functional new phone. You may think, "Oh, that was easy"—but that's because somebody *made* it easy, by doing their job well. The sales clerk isn't expecting a thank-you card in the mail—it's just what they do. They may well celebrate their efficiency in their own way, though, with their friends and family.

All the same, it never hurts to acknowledge somebody for going the extra mile. Even if we know that we're doing something well, it never hurts to hear it. If you're in a restaurant and you get great service, you should obviously reflect that in your tip. Smile and say something friendly to your server, too, though. They're working a job to make rent, but they're also going above and beyond because they care about you enjoying your experience.

On the flip side, if you work in a restaurant and a customer is a jerk to you, let it go. They're probably having a bad day, and they're taking it out on you because they can't yell at their boss, their spouse, or their kids. Take a breath, and ask yourself if somebody else's behavior really matters to you. It shouldn't, as it's their problem. Once you can think that way, you'll stop giving an *F*— and you'll focus instead on the happy, smiling customer at the next table over.

You Know What Matters—Nobody Else

My childhood taught me a lot about what I should and shouldn't care about. My experience was being raised in the Southeast of the United States, which is the Bible Belt. I was supposed to be the very embodiment of the polite young lady—the stereotypical Southern belle.

I was told to stand up straight, cross my legs at the ankles, speak when spoken to, never interrupt an adult—especially if they were male!—and perhaps most importantly of all, never let a curse word pass my lips. Some of those teachings came from my parents and my grandparents, but societal pressure played a big part too. That was simply how a young lady from that part of the world was expected to behave.

Now I am an adult, and I curse like a sailor. Sorry, not sorry. That is *absolutely* unacceptable in the Southeast of the United States. As you may have picked up from this book, though, I don't give an *F*. Obviously I still have standards. If I'm at a restaurant or another public place and there are children around, I'm going to rein it in. That's just basic respect for how other people want to raise their families. F-bombs are not considered to be acceptable in certain company, and I acknowledge and respect this. In the Bible Belt especially, however, you have to mind your language. Any kind of profanity or blasphemy is considered enough to keep you out of heaven. Apparently God keeps a ledger of how many times Laura Casselman uses a no-no word, and that will be counted against me when my time eventually comes.

I have a problem with that—namely, that no god I could ever believe in would behave in such a way. Of all the things going on in the world, I *cannot* believe that God would be concerned if I say, "Sh**, that hurts!" when I stub my toe. My grandmother would beg to differ, and that's fine. I respect her views, and I respect her. As a result, I will not swear or curse when I'm in her company. It doesn't mean that I'm never going to swear in my personal or professional life again though. And, look, I'm not mean to people!

I may have a dirty mouth, but I'm a good person. Surely that balances it out?

Another thing about the Southeast is that women are expected to get married and have babies. Do not pass Go, do not collect $200—that's just the way things shake out once you've finished high school. I'm turning forty this year, and I have not had children. I happen to know now that I would like to be a mother, but I didn't have kids ten, fifteen, and twenty years ago when my friends did. What's important to me is that I do not regret that in any way.

I have always known what is important to me, and when. That's what I have always focused my energy on caring about. If I had kids when I was younger, I'm sure it would have been great. I wouldn't have been a professional dancer, though, and I wouldn't have performed on stage with the Radio City Rockettes, which was my dream since *I* was a young girl. I would not have traveled the world, which I honestly believe has made me a better, happier person.

Those were my choices, and I stand by them. I knew what made me happy, and I figured out what I cared about. Now, I'm ready to figure things out. I may or may not be able to have kids myself. Personally, I'm not opposed to adoption. What I *am* opposed to is being told that, unless I am married and have children, I have no value in this world. You can think that way if you like. That's your right. Thankfully I'm also well within my rights to not give an *F* about your opinion, thank you very much.

Who Cares? *You* Should

As a woman in corporate America, I obviously experience frustrations and struggles in the way I'm treated. I've relayed some examples of this in previous chapters, and trust me, I'll be sharing more in those that follow!

One thing that I often hear from male colleagues is, "I don't know how you put up with that." Well, guess what—I don't know how *you* could watch me put up with that and not speak up. It's everybody's responsibility to care about how other human beings are treated and spoken to.

I have to deal with it by acknowledging what was said or done, weighing it up, and deciding how I'm going to react—if at all. Sometimes the person behaving in an offensive way is so insignificant that I can just brush them off and move on. If you're a small fry and are just acting with ballast and bravado, I don't give an *F*. I'm too busy to validate your ego by giving you the attention you so clearly desire from me.

The irony is, oftentimes the men that attempt to belittle me rank lower in the corporate hierarchy. I know they're looking at me and thinking, "Be quiet, little girl, the men are talking." That's their business. My own thought process is more akin to, "Not your witch with a b."

I don't have to say such things, though, because I know I'm in charge. I know I make the decisions. As a result, it's all water off a duck's back. It's like a dog barking and growling at me. You're acting tough now, little doggy, but you still can't operate a can opener when you're hungry or tickle your own belly. You need me a whole lot more than I need you.

Having said that, there are certain things that do annoy me and that I do care about. A big one is being interrupted by a man—because it's *always* a man—saying, "What Laura is trying to say is . . ."

What I'm trying to say is what I am saying. I know exactly what I mean, and I don't need you to help with that. Not least because you don't *know* what I'm trying to say. You haven't walked my path. I get that some people struggle to get their words out, but that's their battle to fight.

Again, there's a line here. I'm not just Laura Casselman, CEO of JVZoo. I also have a personal life. That line is very clear and direct for me—when I'm at work we're dealing in a business setting, and at home it's a different ball game. If I'm at my parent's house, I'll always respect their opinion. I may not agree with it, and I'll say so if that's the case, but I wouldn't take anything to heart.

Sometimes the lines can blur. In my business, I have to attend a lot of events that are equal parts social and professional. Somebody may approach me and tell me how they think I should be running my business. Again, I'll listen to them and respect their opinion. I can't say that I'll lose any sleep over it, but I'll take it on board. Some people can make me lose all regard for them through their behavior though.

I was at a party a while ago that JVZoo was hosting, and one of the marketers I work with approached me. He was clearly uncomfortable and was wrestling with whether he should tell me what he had heard another guest saying about me. After a little cajoling, he admitted that this other guest—a guest at *our* party, I'll remind you—was bragging to anyone that would listen about how he was only attending because he wanted to *F* me.

God bless this marketer (really). I asked him to stand between me and this other idiot for the rest of the night, and he did just that! Every time this other guy started making a beeline for me, he stepped in. To cap it all, our loudmouthed friend is not very successful in this business. All the same, he felt brazen enough to speak this way about the head of a company his business relies on.

The irony in all this is that the marketer that helped me out had traveled in from outside the country. He uses JVZoo to run his own business, but I do not directly employ or manage him. All the same, he refers to me as his boss. I always tell him that this isn't the case, but he insists that, in the grand scheme of things, I am! He's just being respectful.

That, in a nutshell, is why I give an *F* about him. He respects me and the job that I do within our business. I reciprocate that respect. I can't say the same for Captain Loudmouth, who clearly feels that sipping a few glasses of champagne on our dime gives him the right to behave boorishly. I don't care about somebody so underdeveloped and broad. All I care about is not being trapped in a room alone with him.

Not giving an *F* about things that don't matter doesn't come easy to everybody. Some people are born with the ability. They're the kids who forge their own path, completely indifferent to other people thinking they're weird because they don't fit the mold. It's like being good at a sport or having a natural talent. It's just something they *do*. The rest of us—and I include myself in that—have to work on it.

The most important thing is learning what you should care about. Here's the thing, too—if it matters to you, it *matters*. If you feel you're being mistreated in the workplace because of your gender, don't let somebody, including other women, say, "Oh, that shouldn't matter. You're just being sensitive."

Never let somebody else tell you what should or shouldn't ruffle your feathers. If it matters to you, make it your mission to stop it from happening again.

Personally, I think a lot of men in my business are too sensitive. They seem to grow irate when I speak in favor of female empowerment. They can't seem to understand that I don't want to take anything away from men; I just want to stop female oppression. It doesn't change the fact that it matters to *me* though. Again, they have their view, and I have mine.

We may never agree; such is the way of the world. I don't have to care about their opinion. I'll just keep on doing my thing. As long as you have your priorities straight, it's all good. I know where shoes fall in my list of priorities, and I'm not going to go broke for them. When all my other ducks are in a row, I'll indulge myself—and I won't give an *F* about how much they cost.

Chapter Six

Know Your Strengths

My mother had a class reunion party to attend the other week, which was close to where I live. She had to dig out some materials for it, and while she did so, she found all kinds of memories from my childhood. They were mostly photographs, but there was also a letter I wrote that made us both laugh.

It was a note that outlined the rules of calling a family meeting. We only ever did that if we had an emergency, and it mostly applied to my cousins of a similar age. It transpired that even as an eight-year-old, I was outlining how to go about calling a meeting and who was responsible for what while we were together.

Now, I'm not saying I would lie awake at night dreaming of becoming a CEO while I was in second grade. What this letter showed me, though, is that we're always the same person at heart! We grow and evolve as we go from childhood to adulthood, plus all those awkward stages in between, but I can clearly say that I was always the same deep down.

I learned things about myself throughout that journey. Maybe they were obvious to other people. I'm sure my cousins, who were told in no uncertain terms what was expected of them, had a clear idea of the adult I'd turn out to be! Over time, though, I have really learned what I'm good at. I have also learned that what we're good at doing and what makes us happy are not necessarily the same thing.

I bring up this letter because it reminded me of something important. That learning what we're good at doing, much like learning what we love, begins in childhood. We discussed in a previous chapter how so many adults are unhappy because they didn't take the time to learn this as kids, and I stand by that.

When you're young, you have all the time in the world to discover what flicks your switch and what leaves you cold. When you grow up, there are bills to pay and responsibilities to meet. This means you may have to settle for doing what you're good at, just to make a buck. That's a quick way to turn a carefree kid into an embittered, unhappy adult.

Think Outside the Box

When our strengths make us happy, it's a wonderful thing. It takes a lot of the sting and petty frustration out of life's more challenging moments. However, so many of us are good at things that we're largely indifferent to. Sometimes, what we're good at makes us outright miserable. That's why it's so important to figure out what matters to you. You need to use that information to make the trade between what you're good at and can earn a living doing, and how much time that affords you to do what makes you happy.

I sometimes look at my job with this thought process. I fully acknowledge that I am lucky in that I enjoy my job. Catch me on a good day, and I'll say that I outright *love* my job. Encounter me at

3:00 a.m., cursing like a sailor and trying to put out three business fires at once, and you may get a different response. That's another story for another time though. The question is, can I put my hand on my heart and say that the responsibility of being a CEO makes me *happy*? I don't know if I can.

Again, this isn't a complaint, and you can pack away your violins. I enjoy what I do, and I chose this path for myself. Given the choice to do it all again, I would do it again without a moment's hesitation. Nobody makes me do the things I do, and I'm living life on my own terms. Perhaps more importantly, I'm playing to my strengths.

My role satisfies my need for control. That's not a matter of happiness or unhappiness—that's just a need that I recognize in myself, and I have to meet that.

My role helps me maintain the financial stability that is important to me, and affords me the opportunity to travel—something that *definitely* makes me happy. There are days that I figure stacking shelves at a grocery store would be a less stressful life, but that wouldn't pay for a trip to Europe to see the Northern Lights.

I also know I'm good at what I do. This means I'm not drifting through life, and I'm making a difference. That, more than anything, makes me happy within myself.

Having said that, when I took this job, I opted in for a whole lot of responsibility. That's the gig; big titles come with big responsibilities. Not everybody needs a big title in life, and not everybody needs what I do. That's awesome. I know what I need, though, and that's where the trade comes in.

I can say that when I take a breath and look at all aspects of my life, I am happy. Are there things I would trim out if I could? Maybe. Do I focus on those and question whether I made the right decisions? Never.

On the flip side of this, I have a friend who was a Secret Service agent for a great many years. Now, you don't get to spend a long time in that job unless you're good at what you do, and he was *very* good. If he wanted it, he had a job for life. The trouble was, he *didn't* want that.

The fact was, working for the United States government was making him deeply unhappy. Unfortunately, the better he became at his job, the deeper into the rabbit hole he went. The more time he spent within the government, the more he realized how inefficient they were, and how that conflicted with his personal values!

In the end, he had to walk away. He set up on his own and started a security business, so he could still use his existing skill set. Sure, working for yourself isn't quite as cool or glamorous as being in the United States Secret Service. He has to pay for his own sunglasses now too. That's a joke, by the way. All the same, that coolness had worn off for him. When he weighed his options, that job title was not worth the trade-off of his personal happiness. That meant he had a decision to make. From what I can tell, he made the right call. He seems much more content in his life and work than I have ever seen him before.

Weaknesses Are Fine—Within Reason

When you play to your strengths in life, you're much more likely to be happy. Sometimes it's not that simple though. If your weaknesses—and we *all* have weaknesses—are holding you back, you should look at that.

> Life would be pretty dull if we were all flawless, but that doesn't make self-improvement a bad thing.

At the very least, learn enough to know whether somebody else is helping or hindering you. If you're paying for a personal trainer, you'll be expecting to see results. If the PT in question is seventy pounds overweight and taking cigarette breaks in the middle of your session, you'll quickly realize that you're wasting your time and money. Sometimes, however, the distinctions are subtler.

This is something that I encounter in business all the time. I run a technology company, but I'm not a developer. These are different skill sets that are equally critical to the success of JVZoo. A football team needs quarterbacks and kickers to thrive, and it's rare that you'll find somebody that can do both. The same applies to the world of business.

I don't know how to write code. I don't want to learn. I know that it would not bring me any joy. I mean no offense to developers when I say that, and I'm confident that none will be taken. Survey a hundred developers, and I'm pretty sure you won't find many that would relish the idea of managing budgets or attending meetings for hours. The roles have different skill sets, and they attract different individuals.

So, I'm not a developer. However, I *do* know enough about developing to know who is good and who is not. I know how long something should take and when somebody in my company is being inefficient and wasting time. I know when code is streamlined and effective and when it is needlessly overcomplicated. I can take a look at lines of code and tell a developer when to reel something in or even when they're producing junk that barely functions. I have educated myself enough to be good at what I do, even if I'm not hands-on with every element of it.

On the other hand, there are things I'm *not good* at. Topgolf, for example. For the uninitiated, Topgolf is a social golfing activity. A group of you head to a driving range where you have your own personal bay, and you take turns hitting golf balls toward particular targets. You score points based on where your shot lands. Perhaps more importantly, you get to have some drinks and hang out with your friends.

Now, here's the thing. I'm awful at golf. I'm not being modest or self-deprecating here; I'm *really* bad. Do I care? Not even a little bit. I still have fun playing. That's something I wish more parents would teach their kids.

> You can lose a game and still have fun. You don't need a participation trophy or to be declared the best loser. Take your *L*, suck it up, and ask yourself a simple question: "Did I have fun?"

If the answer is yes, where's the problem? Obviously Topgolf is a flippant example of this, and this rule shouldn't apply to all walks of life. Don't become an airline pilot and crash a commercial jet on the grounds that you had a few laughs while you were at it. Your spare time is fleeting and precious though. You can fill it with things that you're already good at doing, and that's great. If you tackle something outside your comfort zone, that's fine too. You don't have to be an expert at everything.

The first time I ever went to Topgolf was with my nephew. He had never so much as held a golf club in his life before, and he was nervous about it when we started. He still wiped the floor with me though! That's great—he had fun, and so did I. I don't link my value as a human being to my Topgolf ability. I care about spending time with my friends and family and having some laughs. If they get a few extra laughs out of me swinging my club and missing the ball completely, so much the better.

Don't get me wrong—I like to win. Last time I was there and was being mocked mercilessly, I joked that I would hire a coach and train in private. Would I do that? If Topgolf really mattered to me, you know I would! Being good, bad, or indifferent at this game doesn't impact my life in any way though. I would much rather spend what limited free time I have with people who are better at running companies than me, working on side projects, or fulfilling a job that I was hired for to the best of my ability. These are the things that matter to me.

Enjoy Other People's Strengths

It's also OK to look at other people and help them play to *their* strengths. One of my friends is an amazing chef. She's just fantastic. With that in mind, I'm happy to let her take the lead when we're having dinner together. I may need control in most aspects of my life, but when she's cooking I play sous chef and thank her for letting me watch a master at work.

She puts time and effort into cooking because it matters to her. She doesn't cook for a living. She cooks for her friends and family, and that's her love language. That's not necessarily something I do myself, but I sure do enjoy being one of the people who she invites to her house and cooks for!

That makes me feel special, because I know how much it means to her. Nothing warms my heart more than watching people do something they're good at and that they also love. *That's* what makes a person happy. Those are good people to be around. They're not complaining about how unfair life is. They're focusing their energy on bringing positivity into their life, and by extension, mine.

Even when she's not in the best of moods, it works out well for me. When she is feeling blue, is ticked off, or just needs to get out of a funk, she calls me up and offers to cook for me. She knows that's what will bring her happiness and turn her situation around. I don't mind admitting that's a 911 call that I'm always delighted to receive! When I ask what I can bring and she says, "Nothing but wine," that's another win. I know a good wine, and I know how to be a good friend and listen if she wants to talk. That means we're playing to our strengths, and we're both reaping the reward.

I could also learn a lot from my friend, just from the way she does her grocery shopping. She goes through her community sales papers and finds out what's on sale and where. She'll plan her shopping based on what produce is in season and the best possible quality. She'll then come home and plan a whole week's menus around what she just bought.

That blows my mind! If I went shopping without planning ahead, I'd barely have enough to cobble together one meal. My cart would just contain whatever I was hungry for at that moment. She can pull together a refrigerator full of quality produce because the butcher in store *A* had one thing on sale, and the deli counter at store *B* had something else that went with it. My brain just isn't wired that way, and I think it's awesome.

If at First You Don't Succeed . . .

I sometimes look at people in their twenties and think about what a wonderful time of life that is. You're an adult, but not *really*. As the saying goes, you're old enough to know better and young enough not to care. It's a time that you can mess up wildly, as you generally don't have as many responsibilities or expectations, and still have time to pick up the pieces. You get to experiment in your twenties in ways that you can't really do in your thirties and forties.

I'm not saying that your life is over post-twenty-nine. If you still don't know what you're good at when you're forty-two, it's not an excuse to give up. You have to work that out, quickly. Your twenties is just a unique time where you can try new things and learn what you're good at—and what you're bad at. If you bomb big in one company, you can make sure that doesn't follow you to the next. If something blows up in your face, learn why and move on. You have time to figure things out.

Here's some advice for all the twentysomethings reading this book; this is your time! So many people in their twenties teeter on a kind of precipice, feeling that they want to be responsible. They may go clubbing on a Friday and Saturday night to show their wild side, and focus on work the rest of the time.

You have the rest of your life for that. This is your chance to be bold. Go traveling. Do great things. Try new careers and pastimes on for size, and see how they fit. I'm not saying you can't do these things at any age. It's just that when you're still in your twenties, you can make questionable choices and mess things up without ruining your life!

If you're really lucky, you'll learn early what you're good at doing and what brings you joy while you're having these amazing experiences. If that applies to you, capitalize on it! You can use that realization to do good in the world. A prime example of this is Tony Robbins, somebody I admire hugely. If you can ever get to one of Tony's events, I can't recommend it highly enough. If you can't, at the very least read his books or watch his documentary on Netflix.

The way Tony runs his events is different from how I typically live my life. I'm not the kind of person who stands on my chair and high-fives everybody in a ten-foot radius. That's just not my cup of tea. It *becomes* my cup of tea when I'm at a Tony Robbins event though! Suddenly, I'm into it, and it becomes fun. High five!

Changing things up and being adaptable has always been important to me. Ever since I was in my teens and early twenties, I have avoided my comfort zone. I have surrounded myself with people who fascinate me and from whom I can learn. That doesn't mean I find fascinating people uncomfortable. It just means I try to avoid slipping into the habit of only spending time with people in the same place in life as me.

I love the way diverse people think and what they accomplish. I grew up in a very small town, where I graduated from a high school class of eighteen people. I was *supposed* to be a certain way, and I *was* that way for the longest time. There were certain parts of myself that I couldn't make fit into a mold, but for the most part I managed. I wouldn't say that I ever felt like a square peg in a round hole. I made it work.

I always knew that I was destined to leave that small town early though. Even my mom would tell me that I was going to leave as soon as I was old enough. In my thirties however, she kept asking me when I was coming back.

Having said that, my family has always supported me in all my ventures. My mom always wanted me to experience the things she never did. I still remember the first time she drove me to a town that had skyrise buildings. That blew my mind! She had never thought about it, as she'd been in many big cities before.

I always knew I needed the city life. I ended up going to college in the town with the aforementioned skyrises, but after a year, I came to realize that I needed more. I needed *bigger*. That's just me though. My dad doesn't want to be anywhere near a tall building. That's not the existence for him; he built a happy life in a small town for a reason. He wants land, a backyard, and a neighbor that isn't on top of him 24/7.

When I got out into the wider world, I realized how many different characters live in the city and how much I could learn. These fascinating people became my circle and still are to this day. I wouldn't say that I'm on their level, and maybe I never will be. One of my friends does near-constant charity work, while another is an artist. They're achieving great things and leaving a legacy that will be here long after we're all gone. Something about that blows my mind. I've always had a need to surround myself with people who teach me new things, and I'm lucky enough to still call them my friends.

Another important thing about leaving your comfort zone is that people will keep you honest. I have had a heck of a time at work lately, and I haven't been sleeping. As a result, some of my ideas were drying up, and those that I had were not great sometimes. When I'm running on fumes, I'll jot something down in my notebook, then look again twelve hours later and think, "Thank goodness I didn't say that out loud—that is *awful!*"

The trouble with success, however, is that people stop telling you your ideas are awful. I have to be careful not to surround myself with yes-people. Because I have had some great ideas in the past, I sometimes find that people automatically say yes to everything I suggest. It seems that the attitude is, "Well, Laura said it, so it must be great."

Yes, I'm still capable of great ideas—but I still need people to call me out on the ones that are pure BS, especially when I'm too exhausted to immediately tell the difference! That's a strength of character that you'll always need around you.

Dress to Impress

One of my most important tips about understanding your strengths is learning how to play the hand you're dealt. We can all boost our standing in so many subtle and unsubtle ways. The clothing we wear is a prime example of this.

When I worked in sales, I always dressed a certain way. I always loved it when I didn't need to pitch to a female executive, because I knew I could sell any man on anything I needed to. Sorry, men. I love you, but it's true. You're simple creatures at heart.

It didn't matter if the guy was straight or gay. I could always find something to relate to, right off the bat. Sometimes, they would be staring at my legs from the moment I walked through the door. It was pretty clear to me that these clients were not going to listen to a single word I said. They were in the bag, and they were going to be an easy sale. It could have been a gay man, and I could see that they absolutely loved my shoes. Whoever it was, I could find common ground.

Did I get tired of playing those games? Of course I did. I value my brain, and I knew that I had skills and strengths I didn't even need to exercise. It was a means to an end though. I needed to make my rent each month, and I needed to post certain results to climb the corporate ladder. We use the resources we have, even if it's stupid!

The position I'm in now changes things. In fact, it's the opposite. Now, if I want somebody to listen to me, I practically never wear skirts. I'm usually found in a jumpsuit or pants. If I wear a skirt, it will usually come down to my calves or ankles. Usually, if you see me giving a major presentation in a skirt or shorter dress, it's because I spilled coffee all over my outfit in the morning and had to take emergency measures! It's happened!

I find that jumpsuits work for me. Women are not offended by me wearing them and consider them classy. Men don't stare at my legs, and they actually listen to what I have to say. Colors are also really important though. I am *very* intentional about what colors I wear in different situations.

I avoid colors that are generally considered to be unpopular with the masses. There are days when I feel bright and cheery and want to wear a canary-yellow shirt. I resist this, as I know it isn't going to sit right with certain people. Green gets a weird reaction from people, so I typically avoid it. Teal, blue, black, red, and purple—these are the colors that draw respect from people, and what I wear when I want them to like me.

If I'm at a mostly female event, or when I'm not the center of attention and I'm not expected to talk, I'll relax a little. By day two, I won't wash my hair. I'll tie it back and wear a hot-pink shirt if that's the headspace I'm in. It's funny, because those are the days women I have never met approach me and tell me how amazing it is that I'm dressed in fun and lighthearted clothes, like I don't care about what anybody thinks. That's so sweet—I think!

It's true—I don't give an F. We covered this in the previous chapter. All the same, I have to play to the scenario I'm in. I'm not stupid. I know that if I wear a hot-pink shirt and my hair in a ponytail on stage when I'm speaking, I'll lose a portion of my audience. There's a psychology behind color, and some shades are always going to elicit better responses than others.

If I'm going to a meeting that's mostly populated by men and I feel that I have a point to prove, I'll wear red or solid black. They're confident, fearless colors that denote a competent image. If I want people to agree with me, I'll wear blue, as that's a logical and trustworthy color that sets people at ease. These are the things that enter my mind when I'm deciding what to wear in any situation, not what's on-trend in fashion that week.

Don't Let Your Strengths Become Your Weaknesses

If there was one thing I wish I was better at, it's being able to switch off. It's a constant battle for me, and while I'm getting better at it, I'll always have at least half a mind on work. That's just how I'm wired.

Even while I was in Iceland with my parents recently, I was getting up several hours early and going to bed several hours late to check in and stay on top of work. I also made regular phone calls to check in. There is no such thing as a full vacation or a week off work in my life right now.

Cell phones have changed everything. My whole life is on my cell phone. It's how I stay up-to-date with my business and the industry as a whole. Obviously, emails also come and go at lightning speed. There's always *something* that needs my attention, and I can't just let that lie. I may get up and type out a response to an email at 3:00 a.m., even if I'm not sending it until the morning. I'd always rather do those things in the moment than sit on them.

Another big deal for me, and the reason why JVZoo is so successful, is that there is always somebody available to help with an issue. Even though we have a small employee base—the largest our team ever got was sixteen people—we're a huge company. We have over nine hundred thousand users and over eight million customers all over the world. There is always somebody awake, every second of the day, using JVZoo to process sales. This means that somebody is always available to get back to people.

When I look at the social media feeds of our competitors, there are customers complaining that they opened a support ticket days ago and nobody was getting back to them. The response was that it was the weekend and people needed time off. They clearly don't prioritize their users.

With JVZoo, because we have cultivated a reputation of being always available, people bite our heads off if they have to wait thirty minutes for a response. People get acclimated to things, and remember what I said about setting your own bar and jumping to it every day! We have to remind ourselves that we provide a service nobody else does, and you have to pick and choose your battles in life. I chose to be the person who doesn't have much time, and I've made my peace with that.

I'm getting better at taking time to myself, though, and I don't spend *all* of it googling Topgolf coaches. I recently had a Sunday where I closed the curtains, only checked my cell phone twice, and generally took the day off. I was acutely aware that my brain was fried, and I needed that moment to recharge. My next challenge is to claim two full days as vacation, and eventually a week. It's baby steps!

Here's the thing, though: I'm not sure I could ever *completely* switch off. Even if I won the lottery tomorrow and picked up a jackpot that meant the grandkids of my grandkids would never have to worry about work again, I couldn't just walk away. Fear is not an emotion that comes easily to me, but I can say with all sincerity that the idea of being unemployed fills me with horror.

Right now, I can't entertain the notion of not working. I love to travel, and I have no problem sipping a margarita on a beach. I feel like I have *earned* those moments, though, and I cherish them all the more as a result. The thought of doing that all day every day just doesn't appeal. What would be my purpose? What would drive me to put my feet on the floor every morning? How am I going to contribute to the world and change the face of business if I'm not part of it?

I have no issue with people who are unemployed. I know a number of wonderful, talented, and fascinating people who have been out of work for a prolonged period of time, even pre-COVID-19 times. What I can't get on board with is the attitude of, "I'm not taking a job until it's the right role that pays me what I deserve."

What you deserve? What *does* somebody deserve when they haven't worked for years? Life moves pretty fast, especially in my industry. If I didn't work for a year, my finger would be too far from the pulse to really make the impact that I want.

My personal standpoint is that I'm going to work at the level I'm capable of working at, for as long as I'm able. If the time comes that I have to take five steps back, then I'll do that. As long as there is breath in my body and I'm capable of doing it, though, I *will* be working and earning income. That's just who I am. Now. I do, however, reserve the right to evolve and change my mind.

Very occasionally, I'll allow myself a short, unscheduled break. Usually, when I'm crabby about finishing work at 2:30 a.m. with a to-do list that doubled after midnight, I'll still force myself to get up at 5:00 a.m. and attack the new day. Every now and again, I'll let myself get an extra hour of sleep or cool off. For the most part, though, it comes back to what I said earlier in this very chapter: I signed up for this.

Maybe this is why switching off doesn't come naturally to me. Oftentimes, it's just not an option due to unique circumstances. For example, my company was in litigation for two and a half years. If an attorney or the court needed something, they needed it immediately. The moment that ended, my entire industry experienced payment processor problems. If your company can't process payments, they can't make money, and if your company stops making money, they cease to exist. That meant I needed to work several months of nineteen-hour days and maintain a constant state of cat-like awareness just to keep all the plates spinning.

I know people who complain about working a twelve-hour day and how unfair that is. That sounds like a part-time job to me—next they'll be bragging that they had a lunch break! I get that, though, and I've been there. I used to be the employee who worked a twelve-hour shift and witch with a bed and moaned about it. Sales was a nightmare for this. At the end of the month, you'd have to pile on the hours to make those numbers, and I hated that business model. These days, though, I work longer days, usually with a smile on my face.

Trust Your Team

This doesn't change the fact that working such long shifts isn't for everybody. There are people who are equipped to concentrate for twelve hours straight, like soldiers or surgeons. Surgeons can remain focused for an uncanny amount of time, and it's amazing to watch.

Others, like me, know when it's time to step away for ten minutes. It's just important to know when those ten minutes are up and to regain focus and return to your desk by minute eleven. If you don't, ten minutes becomes thirty, which becomes an hour, which becomes a lost day. Time waits for no man, or woman—believe me, I've tried to convince it to!

There is another, larger group of people out there. They're the ones who just can't sustain focus for prolonged periods of time. You might get four hours out of them at a time, and that's that—they won't be producing their best work any longer. That's why I find the corporate structure so frustrating.

Assign somebody an eight-hour shift that involves turning up at X time and finishing at Y time. You won't get eight hours of high performance from them. You just won't. Their attention wanders, and they start phoning it in, whether that's a conscious decision or not. If your company doesn't operate set hours, why restrict your employees?

That's not how I do business. Personally, I could care less how my team arranges their day. I just tell them their deadline, and the days that I have the capacity to check in with them. Beyond that, they're grown-ups who can take responsibility for their own working patterns.

Some people are sharp as a thumbtack in the morning and fade later in the day. Others struggle to pronounce their own name before 11:00 a.m. but come to life in the evening. Some people *like* the structure of nine to five and prefer to work in that format. As long as the work I assign gets done to the schedule I lay out to the standard I expect, it's none of my business *how* it gets done. I have bigger things to worry about than somebody arriving in the office at 9:10 a.m. when their contract says work starts at 9:00 a.m.

Playing to these strengths is an important part of being a leader. So is finding out how people learn and tailoring your communication to that. Some of us are visual learners who prefer to watch videos of live demonstrations. Others find it easier to follow written instructions. I'm a combination of the two, which has caused me some frustration in the past!

My GPA in college was hit by the fact that I didn't always show up to lectures, and they took attendance records (don't even get me started on how dumb I thought that was). The fact was, I attended every lecture for the first few weeks, but they purely consisted of the lecturer reading the contents of the textbook.

OK . . . but I'm pretty sure everybody who was accepted into college could read just fine. I know I could. I could also read a whole lot faster than he could talk. Why would I waste my time having somebody do the reading for me? I'm just going to zone out. It's the same with talk radio for me. While I'm also a visual learner, audio just doesn't cut it for me. Rather than listening to a podcast, I'd rather wait for the transcription.

As a company, JVZoo caters to all strengths in this sense. We have instructional videos for visual learners, and bullet points for those who prefer the CliffsNotes. That's playing to the strengths of our audience and ensuring their needs are met so they can achieve success through our platform. The more popular formats are not always my preference, as research shows that most people prefer instructional videos, and I loathe them. To me, that's a five-minute video teaching me something I could learn in ninety seconds by reading. My strengths are not the same as yours, though, so I make sure we cater to everybody.

Delegating Takes Strength

A while ago, I attended the Stevie Award, which is a ceremony arranged by the American Business Award Association. I was chatting to another female executive there, and she took a call from a personal assistant. People who have personal assistants never fail to astound me, and I had to ask her to tell me *everything* she did to make that relationship work for her. How did she hire them? How did she feel comfortable turning things over to an assistant? How long did it take?

I grilled her for at least ninety minutes and was even more stunned when I found out she had recently taken on a second assistant, as she was getting so much of her life back. I decided I was going to take the plunge and do the same thing the moment I got home. I have twenty-four hours in my day, the same as anybody else, and reclaiming just one or two of those would be a precious gift.

Naturally, though, I wanted to walk before I could run. Rather than bringing in an assistant to work alongside me in my office, I took on a virtual assistant. She came highly recommended, and I called all of her references, which were glowing. She still works for me, and she's amazing. She keeps things organized for me, and it only ever takes me one phone call to get her to understand what I need.

I also took on a local assistant who worked alongside me in the office for a while, but I fired her not long after. I need to get better at letting go of things and allowing someone to help me with errands, etc., but that's a story for another day.

Even having a virtual assistant is hard for me though. I completely understand that I need to relinquish some of the responsibilities in my working life and let people do what they're good at doing. I'm great at helping my team do that! When it comes to breaking off a little piece of my own life though? It doesn't come naturally for me.

Of course, there are also other considerations. Sometimes you need to sacrifice even more time before you can start clawing any of it back. I often consult with other companies and explain to them that they simply don't have the time to do everything and they need to delegate more. The issue with this is, once they find somebody suitable, they need to find the time to train them. If you don't spend an hour teaching somebody how to do something the way you want it, you'll lose two or three hours unpicking their errors and doing it yourself. On top of that, you will have paid them for the privilege of making your day suck just a little more than it had to!

My advice in that scenario is to document everything. That way, if things don't work out, you have everything written down for the next person. That will save you a *lot* of time in the future, as you've already done the hard work.

So many entrepreneurs and people running companies just don't have the time to document stuff though. Oftentimes they discover how to do something as a happy accident, and that's how it's done from then on. In many respects, it seems easier to do it yourself than explain your technique to somebody else.

That puts you at risk though. If you find yourself in a position where you literally *cannot* do something yourself, will your business survive? You could have all the knowledge in the world in your brain. Break both your legs skiing though, and that's useless to the people trying to keep your business afloat while you're stuck in the hospital.

This is why I say to fire yourself every 90 days. If you're repeatedly doing a task that you could document and delegate to someone else, then as the leader of your life and/or a company, it's your job to fire yourself from that task and hand it off to someone else.

That's the crux of success. Know what you're good at, and concentrate on that. When you're not so good at something, find somebody who is and delegate the task to them. If they're good at their job, you'll all sleep better. If they're not, cut them loose and find somebody else who meets your needs.

> **Hire slowly, and fire quickly. If you can get to grips with that, you're the master of your own destiny.**

That's all any of us can really wish for.

Chapter Seven

Collaboration

The cry of, "It's lonely at the top," is often heard from success-ful people. I'll be honest; it's something that I can relate to as a CEO. Anybody who reaches the summit of a particular mountain finds that, when they're left to carry the can and make decisions, it can sometimes be tricky to find support.

This is why collaboration and understanding how to make per-sonal dynamics work are hugely important to me. It's something that I work on tirelessly, in both my professional and personal lives. Like anything that's worth doing, however, collaboration is not always easy.

Never Stop Learning

Arguably the most important aspect of collaboration is guid-ance and mentorship. Before I joined JVZoo, I was the senior vice president of another company. When I came to JVZoo, I was the chief operating officer. That meant that the then-CEO was ranked above me, and that was helpful. It meant that I had a sounding board and somebody who could answer my questions and ease me into the company a little more gently.

One thing I quickly learned, however, is that you sometimes need an additional sounding board from outside your company. That is in no way a criticism of my predecessor at JVZoo. It's just that when you're based within a particular business, you know what your business knows. It's a big world out there, and there is no one-size-fits-all approach to success. As a result, it never hurts to learn how other people approach your industry and the challenges within it. I knew I needed to make some changes at JVZoo, and I was keen to glean any information and experience I could from people who had been down that road before.

Obviously you also need a mentor who has more experience than you. I'm still open to mentoring at this point in my life, but I'm not going to approach somebody who's the general manager of a business half the size of mine. I need to pick the brain of the CEO of a major company that has been doing the job far longer than me. That way, they will have crossed bridges that I'm yet to reach.

With that in mind, I reached out to a number of people who I knew I had solid relationships with. I acknowledged that I needed a mentor to help me be the best COO possible. The response was always the same—"Absolutely. What do you need? Ask me anything. Shall we talk once a month?" That was more than fine for me. I didn't need to check in any more than that. On paper, everybody was delighted to help.

The trouble is, business isn't just done on paper. When the time came to have these conversations, nobody showed up for the calls. This is something Sheryl Sandberg, the COO of Facebook, discusses a lot. I recommend taking a look at her book *Lean In* and checking out her website of the same name.

Sheryl is a goldmine of information, and she made one thing clear to me—it's tough for women in business to get mentors. Obviously I'm speaking in blanket terms here, but I'm prepared to take Sheryl's word for this. In addition to my own experience, she has done a great deal of research. She explains that the inability to secure a mentor is the most common complaint she hears.

Now, I want to make something clear here. I don't think that is *because* we're women. I'm not claiming that men won't give us the time of day or that successful women are not prepared to give anybody else a hand. It's just that when you reach a point of seniority in a business, there simply *isn't enough time*. I get that completely. I do my best to mentor anybody who asks me, but I'm still acutely aware of how much of a commitment that is.

Finding an hour a month in my schedule means sacrificing something else to keep that hour free. If there's an emergency elsewhere in the business—and when you're the CEO of a global company, there's *always* an emergency that requires your attention somewhere!—certain things will fall by the wayside. Firefighting is part and parcel of the job we perform.

For the avoidance of doubt, I'm being metaphorical. Please call 911, not me, if your smoke alarm starts to go off.

Despite this, I think a lot of good men in business will also acknowledge that they don't know what *I* personally face as a female CEO. They'll be able to advise me on implementing a companywide health insurance plan, but they can't explain to me how and why I won't get respect from certain people just because of my gender. They're still trying to figure it out in their company, on behalf of their own female employees. We're still taking our first steps into a new world, and we can't run before we can walk.

Now, a lot of Sheryl's advice on finding a mentor wasn't new to me; the steps she suggested were those I had already taken. All the same, it bears repeating. Don't just cold call a stranger and ask them to mentor you. Time is money. You wouldn't approach a stranger on the subway and ask them to cover your rent for the month, so don't expect a stranger in business to give up their time for you. Find some common ground and establish a relationship first.

The reason I found the reaction strange was that I *wasn't* approaching strangers. I was reaching out to people who I had a relationship with and that I knew respected me. I had shared dinners with these people and got to know their families. That's what surprised me when they didn't show up for our scheduled calls. I would much rather they said from the start, "I'm sorry, Laura, but I really don't have the time right now. Can we try again six months down the line?" I would have understood that completely.

I guess it all comes down to one of the biggest driving forces in my life—directness. If you don't have time, or you're not interested, that's cool. Just tell me that outright, and we can all move on. Promising one thing and delivering another, though, achieves nothing. Save everybody some time by showing your cards at the start of the hand.

Playing Well with Others

Of course, mentoring is only part of the puzzle when it comes to collaborating with others. We all also need to work with external companies, clients, and suppliers to achieve what we set out to do. I learned a long time ago that if I'm to enjoy harmonious working relationships with other people, a tailored approach is the way to go. Find that common ground and build a mutually beneficial relationship.

Sadly, not everybody feels this way. I need to deal with a particular company multiple times a day. I won't say their name, but rest assured, you'll be familiar with them and I'm willing to bet that you use their service. When I'm dealing with this company, no matter who I'm speaking to, the attitude is the same. Sadly, that attitude appears to be, "We're the biggest dogs in this yard, and we can do what we want."

I'm not just talking about an ego-driven senior figure here either. It seems to be a company-wide culture. I could be speaking to a frontline support worker who's barely out of college, and they'll take the same approach. They're rude, they're unhelpful, and they'll pass the buck of blame onto any other business that enters the conversation. It's clearly how they're trained—admit nothing, deny everything, never apologize or offer to fix an issue.

Sadly, I still need to deal with this company if I'm going to run my business. They know this, too—that's why they're so arrogant. However, I have been dealing with them long enough to get to know some of the staff. They know me, they respect me, and they know I'm just trying to do things the right way for my business and my industry.

There are employees who will break the code of conduct by stepping outside and calling me back from their personal cell phones. They can't do that inside company grounds—if they're heard admitting that something is the fault of their employers, they'll presumably be tossed into a gulag and never seen again. They want to help, though, and will do what they can. All I can do is sit back and wait for them to come to me. Sometimes they'll leave the company and ask to work with me.

It's ridiculous that it comes to this, and I can't understand how anybody can feel like a leader when their company culture is coated in such a thick layer of bull, but that's the game I need to play. Sadly, unless there are company-wide changes I really can't see happening, this is how it's always going to be.

Consistency is also important to me when it comes to building relationships. An example of this is when I went to change autoresponders. I send tens of thousands of emails every day. I worked with one autoresponder for years and was viewed as just another cog in the wheel until they realized just how much we were pushing through them. Then they became interested in our business and what we were doing.

I went to leave this autoresponder for another, which turned out to be a great thing. Have you ever let your cell phone contract wind down and started to receive increasingly enticing offers to stay with the provider? That's basically what happened here. The company wanted to fly out and meet with us, really find out what we did, and see how they could serve us better going forward.

That relationship was great—at first. Unfortunately, after a while, my employee who managed that contract started to show me some emails. The person who was effortlessly charming and polite to me was extremely rude and discourteous to her. Apparently she was not deemed important enough to be treated respectfully. That led to what we call in the South a "come to Jesus" meeting—a conversation where this company would see things my way or move along and find another client.

I sat them down and explained that being disrespectful to my team is being rude to my entire company, and by extension me, and I wouldn't stand for it. I don't have the time or patience for that kind of behavior. They could either quickly shape up or ship out—I was happy with either outcome. That's the consistency I demand. Thanks for being nice to me in that meeting and all, but disrespecting one of my team members will not be tolerated.

As I said earlier, though, sometimes you need to tailor your approach to collaboration. JVZoo is an international company, so I deal with a lot of different people from a lot of different cultures.

I have to bear that in mind sometimes, even if it's not something I understand or agree with.

For instance, some cultures simply *do not respect women.* Does that piss me off? Yes, mightily. Do I still need to do business? Also yes. This means I have to approach one of my other executives, both of whom are male, and tell them they need to handle a call. They're not always keen, but sometimes what's between your legs is just as important as what's between your ears.

For the record, my colleagues agree that this is BS. That's sometimes the price of doing business though. People are culturally different. I want to change the world, but I'm well aware I can't do that by forcing my own values on people.

I think that, as Americans, we sometimes forget that—mainly because that's what we sometimes do as a country! We head into countries we think are doing things the wrong way, we attempt to force them into our way of thinking by sticking around, and then things revert to the mean when we leave. Not every culture has the same belief system. We talk about the American Dream and feel that's the only way to live a fulfilling life, but not everybody feels that way.

Dealing with Dissent

In previous chapters, I have talked about how you sometimes need to choose the hills you're prepared to die on. The example I just gave is an example of that. If somebody from another culture won't do business with me because I'm female, then I'll get one of my male colleagues to step in. I just want to get that business done, so I'll bend a little on my personal beliefs and bite my tongue. In public, at least!

I'll only bend so far though. I have very distinct lines I will not cross. In the situation I have just described, where another business has a culturally ingrained distaste for women, I'll never ask a female employee to deal with that. If they're uncomfortable being treated or spoken to in a particular way, I completely respect that. I'll never expect somebody to be made to feel like less than they are just because I asked them to. I'll handle this person if they want me to.

I also find it interesting that some people feel they can tell me how to run a business. I'll always listen to suggestions, as I've mentioned before. That's *all* I'm promising, though—that I'll listen. These people can sometimes get downright vile if you don't jump to attention and take their advice. That's another line I won't cross. I am not running my business to please any one individual, no matter how important they consider themselves to be.

Oftentimes, things are escalated to me. JVZoo, like any company, receives its fair share of nasty, unpleasant, and even abusive support tickets. I don't expect my team to blindly deal with that. I do not subscribe to the theory that the customer is always right and has to be accommodated. Occasionally, the customer is a jerk—sad but true. If one of my employees wants me to step in, I'll do so.

My approach to these scenarios is always the same. I'll give anybody the benefit of the doubt once. If they want to have a conversation, like two mature adults, I'll offer them that and try to find a solution. If they go for my jugular, though, I have no qualms about shutting them down. I'll thank them for their feedback and inform them that a parting of the ways is best for all parties.

Sometimes, what I *want* to say is, "We do not want or need your business—don't let the door hit you on your way out." Unfortunately, that's not professional or constructive! I won't be shy about ending the relationship, though, and I certainly never expect my team to suck it up and accept abuse. It's never acceptable for my employees to bend their moral principles.

Sometimes, however, hostile situations can be resolved by giving somebody an ear. If they feel like their voice is being heard, they'll typically simmer down and we can all move forward. Sadly, some people get the wrong impression. If you give them that ear, they'll misinterpret it and start to grossly overestimate their own importance.

I have seen conversations in private groups where people have said, "I have the ear of the CEO of JVZoo. Tell me your feedback and I'll make sure she acts on it." Here's the thing—I'm nobody's puppet. All I'm saying is, "Thank you for your feedback. Message received. I hear you."

"I hear you," is one of my favorite sayings. It doesn't mean that I'll be doing what you've asked; it means that I've listened to what you have to say. I've been using that line on my mom since I was a teenager, so I know how powerful it is!

Sorry, Mom! It doesn't mean I'll be making life or business decisions based on what you've said. It means I've heard what you have to say. Sometimes there's a further conversation to be had, or research to be done, and sometimes it's better to just part ways.

Manage Your Network

Naturally, social media has changed how we communicate and collaborate. Bad news always travels faster than good news, negativity loves company, and cancer spreads if it's not removed.

The accessibility and opportunity to reach the CEO of a company that social media provides is theoretically a positive thing. It's very much a double-edged sword though. If I respond, it *could* be great. The person I speak to goes away happy, and we all move on. On the other hand, it could give the impression that my company is small, or I'm not doing my job properly, because I have the time to address people on social media.

Naturally, though, if I *don't* respond, people will think I'm locking myself away in an ivory tower and consider myself too important to engage. It's interesting to see people's perspectives, but it can sometimes feel like a no-win situation.

Of course, the rise of the online world means we also have to deal with our old friend the keyboard cowboy. From the safety of their computer screen, likely in another state or even another country, people feel they can say things they would never dream of saying to my face. Shoot, they wouldn't even say these things if they picked up the phone and spoke to me.

Narcissism has grown exponentially since the rise of social media, and everybody thinks that what they want matters, and their demands should be met *right now*. As a result, they'll share their every thought, feeling, and emotion on social media. If people don't agree, they'll attack them until they yield.

I'll be honest—I find that scary. We now have a world filled with people who don't know how to handle their emotions or, worse, don't feel the *need* to. Social media can create an echo chamber where you can choose to surround yourself with people who agree with your every word.

Even worse, humans still live by a pack mentality. If one of their friends is putting the boot into a stranger online, there will never be a shortage of people willing to join in too. Kids are committing suicide because of the bullying they're experiencing on social media, reading page after page of comments nobody would ever dare say to their face. That kind of cyber-bullying is cowardice in its purest form.

I have a small number of people online who don't like me. They don't know me, and they have never done any business with me. However, someone I did know told them not to like me, and that was enough for them. This was years ago, but every now and again I give an opinion when asked and find myself attacked by this small pack of hyenas.

I find that fascinating. I have never exchanged words with any of these people, cross or otherwise, yet years later they're still doing somebody else's bidding. That person is out living their life, while these puppets are sitting there waiting for me to say something. That's not a lifestyle that appeals to me, but to each their own I guess. Thankfully, for the most part, this industry moves too quickly to hold a grudge. Somebody may be like a dog with a bone for six months, but they'll move on when there's business to be done.

I work in the tech sector—I get contacted on social media. It comes with the gig. On the same hand, that means that I could easily reach out to the CEO of another company and tell them what a terrible service they provide. I'm sure there are a raft of other people who find them equally distasteful and would relish the chance to pile on once I raised my head above the parapet. That's not how I want to do business though.

Another problem with social media is that when something goes wrong in an industry, everybody wants to have their say on it. They tweet and post, and Instagram and WhatsApp groups start sprouting like weeds. That damages the entire ecosystem of the industry as potential customers see that pettiness. Naturally, they think they wouldn't dare buy from these people. I gave a talk on this for an event in Ireland. People who bad-mouth others within our industry are cutting off their nose to spite their face, just because they have to publicly share their every feeling in the moment.

The fact is, social media is almost entirely ego-driven. Everybody wants their attention and their moment in the spotlight. People are less and less interested in finding a solution; they'd rather make sure everybody focuses on their problem.

You can tell when someone isn't getting the reaction they want because they'll suddenly make twelve negative posts in a day. It's textbook attention seeking from people who don't know how to find happiness in their own skin. They can't build their own business, so they want to tear down somebody else's. They're just sitting behind a keyboard and complaining. Ironically, these are the kind of people who feel it's appropriate to send me or other executives emails telling us how to run *our* businesses! Those are the people who are told, "Thank you for your feedback. We hear you."

It's OK to have emotions. It's important. The trouble is, we're living in a time where we're told that everything we feel is great and wonderful. It is—that's what makes us human. That doesn't mean it's OK to act on our every emotion though. It's not OK to lash out at somebody else because you're angry. We seem to have stopped teaching this in our culture of participation trophies and instant emotional gratification. We have stopped explaining that it's OK to be upset and disappointed, and that you can't win every time.

Disappointment is *great*. Not in the moment, obviously—but it teaches us so much. It helps us understand what is important to us. So you didn't win an award for gaining straight-A grades this semester. Does that drive you to study harder next time and make sure you get what you want? Or is the occasional B a sacrifice you're happy to make, if it means you can let off some steam and go to a party on Saturday night?

Either of those is fine. What's not fine is expecting your parents to march into the school and tear a strip off your teacher, demanding that they change your grade, as you didn't get what you wanted. That will not prepare you for adult life.

When you don't get the promotion at work you were pinning your hopes on, you need to ask why. Did somebody else go that extra mile that you didn't? If so, learn from them and make sure you can't be ignored next time. If not, and you genuinely feel bypassed, it's time to start looking for something else where you'll be recognized and rewarded. Lashing out because you don't know how to handle disappointment isn't helpful to anybody.

Shared Values Are Pivotal

When I think back to 2014 and 2015, it was more than just a heyday for my industry. It was like a different business. There were fewer laws and governing regulations. People were making all kinds of promises. I sometimes hear people now harken back to the "glory days" of 2015 when we all made seven figures with every launch, but we're more closely regulated now. Laws progress as businesses become more commonplace.

One thing I find interesting is that some people in my industry take a more relaxed attitude to the law! They take a pick-and-choose approach to the regulations they're going to follow. I can't count how many times I've told people that what they're doing is illegal, only to be told, "Oh, that's OK, Laura, people don't care about that." Newsflash—I do! JVZoo is compliant with all laws and regulations surrounding the industry. We don't bury our heads in the sand and ignore laws because the industry "doesn't really care about that."

The global nature of my business also makes this interesting. Europe tends to pass laws faster than the United States, and we often play catch-up. GDPR is a big example from recent memory. Once Europe passed that regulation, California quickly followed with the California Consumer Privacy Act, and we saw a trickle-down effect through the US. When VAT became an option, a lot of States opted into that on their online sales. When Europe introduces new legislation, we pretty much know it's coming worldwide.

Having said that, there are still some countries where the internet is essentially the Wild West! There are some nations I deal with who are clearly used to taking things into their own hands. They'll message me saying, "I know who this person is and that they're in the United States. I now need their IP address and home contact information." I don't know what the heck they're planning to do with that information, but I'm sure not handing it over—even if I was legally allowed to do so!

This is why it's so important to do your due diligence before entering into any kind of business relationship. I will never approach anybody unless I know for sure their business and reputation are rock solid.

Recently, I have been looking at payment facilitators so we can remunerate our affiliates as effectively as possible. We've made some great collaborations with companies, some of whom have approached JVZoo directly, saying, "We have never done this, but we see potential here. Can we sit down together and figure something out?" That has led to some really cool ideas that will be industry-firsts when we roll them out. That's the fun stuff.

Sometimes, I even get an email from a third party. They'll say, "I've been watching the way you run JVZoo for the last few years, and I'd like to introduce you to another company, as I think your values are aligned. I don't know if there's anything you can do together, but I think it's worth you meeting."

Overall, that's what matters most—that you share a mutual respect with a collaborator, and you want to do business the same way. They're going to do what they do, and you're going to do what you do. If you can both benefit from that, great.

I'm not saying you'll never butt heads, but if you're not sharing the same office space, you can figure things out. Get contracts in place so you're both protected, and plan your divorce, so to speak. The smartest thing you can do is plan what you'll do when the time comes to part ways, if that's going to be the case. That can be a smooth transition, or it can be an ugly, messy break-up that involves the courts. You have the ability to prevent the latter from transpiring by taking appropriate action at the start.

The only thing that pisses me off in a business relationship is a company not doing what they're supposed to. I'm working with another business right now, and I've had to speak to them about their representative repeatedly not turning up for calls when they're scheduled.

Things happen—I get that. People forget, calendar reminders can fail to pop up, personal and professional emergencies can arise. When it's a repeated mistake, however, it's not misfortune. It's bad planning, and it's not respecting my time. This representative keeps cancelling on me five minutes before we're due to speak, leaving me juggling my time and trying to find when I can fit him in again.

Eventually, I told this representative it was time to put his big boy pants on and come to work. He was very apologetic, but ultimately my time is more valuable than his apologies. I was working to accommodate his requests, and he had failed to do the same too many times.

The most recent incident took place on a public holiday. I planned my day to come into the office when *he* wanted to talk, and he canceled again. His time is not worth more than mine, and it shows a lack of respect for the business collaboration we're forging. I can always tell when he's traveling, as that's when this becomes a repeated behavior. He'll clearly plan to get to the airport early and find a place to speak, fail to do one or both of those things, and try to reschedule. I don't have time for that, especially when the call was only scheduled twenty-four hours before. It's time for a "come to Jesus" meeting, friend!

As long as people are respectful, that's all I want. We don't need to sit around a campfire and sing "Kumbaya" to do business together. I have great professional relationships with plenty of people who I have no interest in sharing a cocktail with outside of work. If we do what we say we're going to do and hit our timelines, I'm happy.

Get to the Point, and Stay in Your Lane

As I have mentioned before, I am crazy direct. One of my biggest challenges is learning how to approach a situation from the side rather than head-on. I don't want to waste anybody's time and get straight onto the nuts and bolts, which some people think lacks finesse.

I'm sorry, but nothing annoys me more than talking about the weather! Unless there's a tornado coming that will destroy one or both of our homes, that holds no relevance to me. I'll play the game, but the entire time I'm running through the whole thing in my head. "It's been thirty seconds, is that long enough, and can we now get to the point?" "No, I need to keep going for another two minutes."

Granted, there is a time that everybody is braindead. I include my company in that. There will be moments when we all realize that we've stopped making sense, so we'll take a few minutes to chitchat (just not about the weather, please) and see if that sparks something. Sometimes, we may even decide that the ship has sailed for the day and it's time to go home and pick up in the morning. That's fine too. We're all aware that after a good night's sleep, we'll have work to do and chit-chat will cease!

Ultimately, collaboration should be a matter of everybody bringing their specialty to the table. I don't understand why so many people have a problem with staying in their lane. The most successful partnerships involve one business or individual doing what they're best at and the other bringing their skill set.

These collaborations then break down when somebody wants to change lanes and start telling somebody else how to do their job. That's just your ego acting up. Stay in your lane! Questions, and an outside perspective, are fine. Just don't muscle in on something that isn't in your wheelhouse. If you don't like the game, then change the rules. Over time, you'll find that you don't need to do that. If a partnership is right, you'll find that the rules naturally change along with you.

Finally, if a collaboration isn't working out for you, cut that cord as quickly as possible. It's the same philosophy as hire slow, fire fast. I've moved to that point in my life in general—personally as well as professionally. I don't necessarily hire slowly in that regard. I'll invite people into my life if they show the appropriate respect to me. The moment I see a red flag though? You're out.

I just don't have the time for that. Your drama is yours, and I just don't care—I'm busy enough with my own problems! I've always been protective of my bubble, and I've always been careful about who I introduce to my family, as they're the kindest, most loving people I know. I've now reached a point where I protect myself to the same extent I protect my family.

I think that's typical for people with a personality like mine, a mothering nature that wants to take charge but nurture at the same time. I certainly spent a long time thinking about how I formerly believed it was OK for certain things to happen to me because I could handle them and they wouldn't scar me. I'm past that phase now though, and I love it! Why did I think that because I *could* handle it, I *should*?

This is why constantly evaluating and working on yourself matters.

> Sometimes you truly have to check the damage, realize it's self-inflicted, and get yourself on a better path.

Each time you do this, you'll be grateful you did.

Chapter Eight

Staying Positive During the Sh** Storm

When I was young, I ran away from home. That sounds dramatic, so I should probably clarify something. When I say, "I was young," I was somewhere in single figures of age.

I don't remember the ins and outs of the situation. I just recall being mad at my parents, muttering how nobody understood me, and packing a bag. As I say, I can't remember what they did to provoke such a reaction. It must have been serious though. As we all know, nobody under the age of ten has ever made an irrational decision.

I made it less than half a mile down the road before I realized this was the dumbest thing I had ever done. I had no idea what I was going to do for dinner that night or where I was going to sleep. Worst of all, I had to carry that bag all the way back home!

I bring this up because that experience was something of an eye-opener for me. When I cut through my anger, it made me realize how grateful I was for everything I had. I had a roof over my head, I had parents who took care of me and kept me safe . . . Suddenly I realized just how lucky I was and how much I had to be grateful for.

This is something I have always been very good at doing. Maybe my upbringing has something to do with that. As I've mentioned in a previous chapter, I grew up in the Bible Belt. I attended church on Sundays as a kid, and I was raised to say my prayers and thank God for everything I had.

Whatever the reason behind it, I have never lost sight of how important the traits of gratitude and positivity are.

> **Being grateful for what we have is the key to remaining positive during a sh** storm.**

And believe me, when you're the CEO of a company, sh** storms rain down on you considerably more often than you'd like!

Let's be clear about something before we go any further. Stopping to smell the roses before dealing with a situation isn't always an option. I'd love to say that I constantly channel my inner Dalai Lama and shrug my shoulders in the face of adversity. That's not the case though.

Sometimes, when there's a fire blazing around you, the only option is to put that fire out. Self-reflection has to wait until that's done. Thinking, "Well, only *half* the building is burning down. I'm grateful for the half that isn't," will not get you very far.

After the event, however, is a great time to take stock. Sit down, think about why something happened, and muse on what you can do to prevent it from happening again. Did you miss something? If so, was it something you *could* have caught?

It's easy to beat ourselves up for not being psychic. Sometimes, though, you have to accept it. Tell yourself, "OK, that sucked. Maybe I could have done more, maybe not. At least I have learned from the experience. Now is the time to rebuild."

That rebuilding stage is the most important part of all. You need to be able to separate yourself from the past and look to the future. I've said before that self-belief and cheerleading is an inside job. After the crap hits the fan, you need to take a moment to take a breath and acknowledge that you have the chops and the chutzpah to put right what once went wrong.

When Managers Become Leaders

When you reach a certain level of a corporate hierarchy, crises become a regular occurrence. When you're lower on the totem pole, you can always toss the ball to a superior and let them handle an issue.

Once you reach the top, however, you realize there's nobody left for you to turn to. That's when you need to keep a cool head and look for the positives among the tidal wave of drama that's heading your way.

How people in positions of workplace seniority deal with a crisis in the corporate world is a great way to tell a manager from a leader. These are two very different roles, with very different skill sets.

One type of person will see a fire blazing and demand to know who started it, allowing the building to burn down around them while fingers are pointed and blame apportioned. Others will concentrate on putting out that fire, understanding that the inquest can wait until the dust has settled. The latter is a genuine leader. The former? Not so much.

So many people in positions of leadership tend to forget that actually *leading a team* is part of the gig. It's not all about the paycheck, the corner office, and the company car. Those perks are great—but they come with a degree of responsibility. Ultimately, you carry the can for anything that goes wrong with the team of people beneath you.

If an employee at JVZoo royally screws up (thankfully that's a rare occurrence!), it's my fault. This could be because I hired them in the first place, erroneously entrusting them with the fortunes of the business, or because I didn't spot warning signs and let them go before damage could be done.

If that sounds draconian, don't be misled. Part of the reason I am where I am is because I take leadership, and the responsibilities involved, seriously. If an employee makes a mistake, I'll deal with it in the moment and then arrange to coach them afterward. We're all human—mistakes happen.

If the same problem arises again, it's time to review the coaching. Did they implement everything they were taught? If so, maybe the coaching approach needs to be amended. A third time though? No, sorry. Not in my company. Three strikes and you're out. I'm a busy woman. I don't have time to hold your hand and do your job for you. That's what I pay you for.

There are exceptions to this rule. If somebody makes a drastic error or misjudgment, sometimes the only option is to let them go immediately for the good of the business. There is a difference between somebody being coachable and outright dereliction of responsibility.

You have to assess whether it was a mistake that anybody could make. If that's the case, institute training so it doesn't happen again. If it was a lack of care or disregard of responsibility, however, there's no coaching that out of people. If somebody thinks it's OK not to turn up to work because they'd rather go to the beach, why do they deserve a second chance? They're showing their priorities are not aligned with mine or those of my business.

Part of my role as a leader is to assess these situations on a case-by-case basis. I never enjoy firing people. I always need to do what is best for the company though. If I leave somebody in their position because I don't want to deal with firing them that day, and they go on to wreak further havoc with bad decisions that impact the rest of my team, that's my fault. I didn't put that fire out, which means that by default I allowed it to spread.

Carrot or Stick? The Eternal Dilemma

As I have covered in previous chapters, I consider positivity to be hugely important. There's a fine line to walk in the workplace, though, especially as a woman. If you're too positive all the time, people don't take you seriously. I learned this the hard way.

I believe I have become better at managing this. Previously, I was a little too extreme, on both sides. I'm a nice person, and I want my team to be genuinely happy in their jobs. I'd do what I could to facilitate that. Unfortunately, it became clear that every time I gave an inch, certain people would take a mile. They were stepping all over me. That inspired me to think, "Huh, two can play this game. Let me show you what *I* can do!"

Thankfully, I learned how to balance this out during my middle management days. I honestly think it's something that everybody has to go through themselves, to find their sweet spot.

Here's an example: the other day, an ongoing issue in my company reared its unwelcome head. A while ago, one of my team made a mistake. OK, it happens. Let's review, see what went wrong, apply protocols to ensure that it doesn't happen again, and we can all move on as better people for the experience.

Then the same mistake happened again—only this time, it was ten times bigger. *Now* I have a problem with this. Once is a mistake. Twice is unacceptable carelessness. That was the message I sent out to everybody working on the project, summoning them to a call to discuss what happened.

My response was pretty simple and direct: "Here's what happened last time. Here are all the steps we put in place to prevent it from happening again. Here's how and where it happened again—all because every preventative step I had put in place was skipped."

I'm not going to stand for that because it suggests somebody simply *does not care enough*. I made it clear that I was going to have to take the project over for myself until my trust was earned back. Because, obviously, I have so much free time on my hands. I was looking for something to fill those pesky two hours I had earmarked for sleep.

I was pretty angry. I'm quite sure that I dropped the F-bomb, which is rare for me in a business setting—at least, it's rare for me to say it in anger! I heard the voice of the employee I was speaking to start to shake, and I let that happen for a few minutes. Afterwards, I softened my tone a little. I explained that I understood that she wasn't sitting at home, cackling maniacally and plotting to single-handedly destroy the company. All the same, it was carelessness and skipping steps which led to this situation. That could not become a habit.

I don't know what was going on that day. There may have been an emergency that distracted everybody's attention. I understand that better than most. If that was the case, though, all the team had to do was ask for help. Choosing not to, and skipping steps instead, led to carelessness. Carelessness was why we were having this conversation.

I ended the call by ensuring this employee knew that I didn't think she was conspiring against me and that I didn't dislike her as a colleague or a human being. All the same, I made it clear that she was an adult who was paid to do a job, and she *didn't* do that job. I just couldn't allow three strikes on this one, and I had to step in. It had happened twice, and if it happened a third time, JVZoo would look like idiots in front of the public. As a CEO, I cannot allow that to happen.

Every now and again, people try to take the, "I didn't know *how to do* that, so it's not my fault," line of defense when things go wrong. Unfortunately, it tends to come up whenever it's a really basic and elementary task. JVZoo is a tech company—that's at the core of what we do. If you can't perform a basic task that my nephew performs on his iPad as an educated thirty-something professional, I don't understand why you'd even apply for this job. That's a BS excuse, and we both know it's a lie.

Why waste your time and mine by spinning that yarn? If you were lazy and didn't follow the protocol, just admit it. I have more respect for that than a ridiculous excuse that holds no water. That's like claiming your dog ate your homework when I know full well your only pet is a goldfish.

Accept Imperfections and Regain Control

If there's one thing in business communications I can't abide by, it's misspellings. Sure, if you're shooting an email off to your teammate, then it's no biggie. Who cares—nobody is grading your communications like a term paper. If an email is going to a client, though, or a marketing piece? Check it, double-check it, and get somebody else to lend an extra pair of eyes. There is no excuse for such basic mistakes.

Now, having said that, I have made that mistake myself. I remember once I was looking at a communication I had spent hours editing. I was so concerned with getting the message right that I made a spelling error in the copy myself. I was mortified, and I took the time to send it to my team with a mea culpa. I pointed out where I had dropped the ball, it was on me, and that's why we should always have an extra pair of eyes. I learned from that incident.

None of us are faultless. We all have flaws, and that's great. Well, sometimes it sucks, but I'm sure that a perfect world would be pretty dull! I wanted to take ownership of my mistake though. I wanted my team to know that I make errors, too, and more importantly, I'm prepared to take ownership for them and make sure they don't happen again. *That's* leadership.

I have discussed in a previous chapter that we can learn a lot from failure and mistakes. It's also OK to wallow a little after we mess up. Sometimes that's a good thing, as it renews our focus and determination not to make the same mistakes again. Just set yourself a time period before you need to put it behind you and re-engage with the world.

Sometimes, after a problem arises that I feel responsible for, I'll sit with it for a while. I'll spend the night thinking it over with a glass of wine and some takeout, questioning myself and pondering what I could have done differently. When the sun rises in the morning, though, it's time to move on. I'll go for a run, get my head straight, and move on. Nothing else can be achieved by thinking about the past. It's gone, and the consequences will be what they are.

Running is how I stay positive and center my personal zen. You may have your own techniques. Speaking for myself, exercise is hugely important to me. It releases endorphins and clears my head. From my perspective, if you're running five, six, or seven miles and thinking about anything other than putting one foot in front of the other and breathing, you're not running hard enough!

That's why exercise is important to me. It's the one time I'm not overthinking. Ordinarily, my mind is like a computer with dozens of Internet browser windows open at once. I can't sleep at night because I have too many thoughts to process. While I'm engaged in a workout, that all goes out the window. Even if it's just for a blessed half hour, and even if I'm working out in the office. After I have taken the time to myself, I think better because my brain has reset. You need to know what helps *you* feel positive, and work toward maintaining it—even when it feels like all is lost.

As you'll know by now, I am a classic type A personality. I need to feel like I'm in control of my life and my destiny at all times. Unfortunately, when the sh** storm hits, that's not always an option. That's the abiding, unstinting thing about a crisis. It makes us feel like we have no control over the chaos that is unfolding around us. If we did, it would just be a minor inconvenience.

Here's the thing though.

When something unexpected happens, we're not powerless. You may not be able to control a situation, but you can control your reactions to it. That's what I always remind myself when something goes surprisingly awry. I am in charge of my own destiny.

I'm no longer that kid who tried to run away from home. I have the power to change the direction of any given situation, all by managing my reaction to it.

I think this is where a lot of people go wrong. They focus on that feeling of powerlessness. They think, "I can't make other people see things from my perspective," or, "I can't make my boss see my worth and give me a raise."

Maybe you can't—but you *can* change how you react to it. Clear your mind, weigh whether you are genuinely being mistreated, and look elsewhere. Find another job, working for people who will see what you can offer. End a relationship if it's no longer fulfilling your needs. Pack your bags and move to a new town—or even a different country—with different opportunities. Just don't bang your head against the wall and gnash your teeth about how powerless you are. That becomes a self-fulfilling prophecy.

The Power of Positivity

Contrary to what you may be thinking, I don't think it's realistic to be positive about everything all the time. Personally speaking, people who have an unflinchingly positive disposition make me nervous. I see them as a ticking time bomb of repressed emotion. When they blow, it's going to be disastrous for everybody in their radius.

What *is* important is taking negative thoughts and attempting to turn them around. If something goes horribly wrong, your first thought may be, "I should have seen that coming." That's fine— maybe you should have. Sit with that for a while, think about it, and question what you could have done to prevent it. Like I said, a little soul-searching can go a long way. Maybe you took your eye off the ball, or you ignored warning signs that should have been obvious.

What *doesn't* help is repeating, "I should have seen that coming," as a mantra and doing nothing about it. No matter how many times you repeat those words, you can't go back in time and change things. You can't go back and see what was unseen, decide not to hire a particular person, or change your mind about taking on a troublesome job or client.

Accept that certain things that enter our lives are negative. You wouldn't be in the midst of a storm if they weren't. We'd choose a fluffier name, like a *glitter cloud*. Accept those negatives, but acknowledge that you have the power to change them. Take positive action, and get yourself out of the mess you're in. No amount of waiting it out will help—things won't automatically turn around. You need to grab the bull by the horns, look that issue in the eye, and remember that you're the master of your domain.

That's one thing I value very highly. I'm never going to be a damsel in distress that waits for somebody else to step in and rescue me from a bad situation. I always back myself to get out of a tight spot.

Obviously, I don't look forward to bad things happening. That's self-loathing, and as we established back in Chapter 1, I actually like myself. I have, however, ensured that I was capable of taking care of myself and my own problems since I was a teenager, though, and there's a great deal of inner strength that comes from knowing I'm capable of that.

People should always be able to trust themselves. We all need to know that when push comes to shove, we can look in the mirror and say, "I got this." That doesn't mean we always get everything we want. It *does* mean that we know we'll survive the storm, though, and figure out what to do next. It may take work, but you'll get through it.

In my business, things can change in an instant. Take payment processing as an example. I discussed my challenges with that in the last chapter, and sometimes the goalposts shift so much overnight that we're basically playing a different sport by the morning.

It would be nice to get a heads-up before that happens, but it's just not how my world works.

When something like this unfolds, it's all hands on deck and panic stations. It can sometimes take as long as six months to untangle all the knots and kinks that have suddenly appeared. I know I'll get through that—but it's still exhausting. Three weeks of sleepless nights into that period, and I'm tired. Three *months* in, I'm feeling like the walking dead. It doesn't change the fact that I have to manage the situation though. I have a responsibility to my team to deal with the sh** storm, because they're relying on their paycheck to feed their babies.

Of course, I also need other people to step up, grit their teeth, and paint on a smile at times. There's an increasing attitude in today's society, especially from the generation that's entering the workplace now, that we should all get what we want at all times, that throwing a tantrum and demanding special treatment is an appropriate response to disappointment and setbacks. I'm sorry, but it's simply not true.

The Western world may be placing more emphasis on emotion and feelings, but that's not a universal trait. There are people—and entire cultures—out there that *do not give a crap* about you or your feelings. They will run roughshod over you in an instant. If your feelings get hurt in the process, that's your cross to bear. You were in their way, and that train wasn't stopping. It's up to you to climb aboard or get off the tracks.

People who do not understand how to deal with the real world and manage their emotions worry me. It scares me to think that sooner or later, they'll be spearheading the workforce. We've previously established that as long as there is breath in my body and I'm capable of doing so, I'll work. Eventually, though, that won't be the case. Who is going to take over roles like mine?

I'm not saying that I'm unique and irreplaceable—far from it. I have no doubt that there are plenty of mini Laura Casselmans out there already. I'm talking about the three-year-olds who won't allow their mom to dress them because they already know their own mind. I'm thinking of the ten-year-olds who get up before school to practice their music and review their homework without being told to do so by their parents. I'm picturing the teenagers who are questioning their teachers rather than passively accepting what they're told and dreaming of the big city and all the opportunities such locations provide. The trouble is, these people are becoming the exception rather than the rule.

The cream will always rise to the top though. In the future, that will be the people who understand how the world is indifferent to them. I worry that they'll be flanked by masses of people who don't get why all supermarkets are self-checkout and we order our food from a computer in the restaurant. There are fewer and fewer jobs every day because busy consumers don't want to deal with other people's nonsense, and employers don't want to pay a salary to somebody who will not bring them any value. The sooner we all accept this, the better the world will be.

Positivity Leads to Change—and Change Can Be Tough

The good news is that anybody can change their approach to life. Adopt a more positive outlook in general, and you'll find it easier to control negativity when it arises. The bad news is that positivity doesn't come naturally for some people. Misery loves company, and you may find that the people around you respond unhelpfully to any change in your attitude.

This may relate to friends, colleagues, or even family members. The people who are supposed to be on your side may start laughing at you, making fun of you, and trying to keep you in the box that you've been assigned. In those circumstances, tough though it may be, you have to treat them like an ex. You don't have to be mean or bite back with hurtful comments. Just treat these people as a part of your past and move on with no ill will.

I have an ex who periodically manages to contact me, and he *always* harps back to a job I had eons ago. He never fails to tell me that role is who I am and who I'll always be. That's just not true. It's who I *was* then, and it played a big part in making me who I *am* today. I didn't stop growing and learning, though, and I hope I never will. He's fond of comments like, "Look at you, Miss Equality-Driven Leader. What a joke you are."

To me, the only joke is that he has the time and inclination to track me down and send those messages. I don't have to tell him that though. I don't have to tell him a darn thing—I delete the message and move on with my day. I know he's acting this way because he is still trapped in that same spot in life. I've long since evolved and moved on.

Twenty years ago, did I think I would consider it so important that women understood they could work in science and technology companies? Not at all. I hadn't gone through what I've been through now, I hadn't grown, and I hadn't dealt with men expecting a BJ in exchange for the paycheck I earned by making money for their company.

So some people may not be supportive when you decide you've had enough and it's time for a change. If they're stuck in a rut, they may not like to see somebody else take a step forward. That's cool. Wish them well and move on. Treat them like an ex.

Say No to Negativity

In the previous chapter, we discussed how bad news travels fast and can spread like a cancer. The same goes for relentless negativity, in both our personal and professional lives. It's so important to cut a cancerous person out before they can infect an entire group of people.

In the workplace, I'll always attempt a coaching approach first. If somebody is unhappy, I want to know why. I'll do what I can to help change that, within reason. What I *don't* want is to hear them complaining and moan in the office. If you want to go home and complain to your spouse, or your friends, or your mom, then all power to you. If they're prepared to listen to your daily sob stories, that's great for you.

I don't want to hear it though. The fact that you're busy and are working long hours doesn't make you special or unique. Everybody is in the same boat. The rest of us just spend more time steering that boat, so we can start claiming back time for ourselves. If these people spent less time telling everybody how much work they have to do and more time actually crossing things off their to-do list, they'd be astonished at how much they could achieve.

I've seen this too many times. People gather around the water cooler, start complaining, and before you know it, there's a fungus of pessimism and low morale taking over a business. If the instigator of this is dealt with, it sends a message to everybody else. Oftentimes people feel much better without somebody in their ear, bringing them down every day. If they don't and they're still miserable, that's on them. Maybe it's time to look for another job. Clearly we come at life from two very different approaches.

It's tough, though, because misery is arguably the ultimate shared experience. Watch a comedy movie in the theater, and maybe half the audience will laugh. Humor is subjective, and maybe they're not in the mood to have a good time. Screen something like *Titanic* or *Field of Dreams*, though, and there won't be a dry eye in the house by the time the credits roll.

You may have experienced this mentality while you're out with friends. You're in a restaurant, having dinner, everybody is having a good time . . . and then the tone changes in an instant. Maybe somebody tells a funny story about a disastrous blind date they just had with a guy that spent the entire meal boasting about how he has the hairiest back in his state. Everybody laughs, everybody starts sharing their own similar experiences.

It only takes one person to change the entire mood. A series of funny stories can become a cautionary tale pretty quickly if somebody fails to read the room. Then, before you know it, everybody is in a funk. That's the point where somebody needs to step up and announce a subject change. If you fail to alter the trajectory, the entire night will become a maudlin endurance test.

Some days, that's acceptable. If you're at a funeral, nobody expects you to fire off your best one-liners and encourage people to turn their frown upside down. Outside of that though? I'm sorry some guy stood you up on Friday night. I honestly am. That doesn't mean all the men in the world are despicable jerks. Let's talk about something else. By the way, I should probably mention that my closest girlfriends are probably reading this and thinking back to times they heard me complain for hours about a bad date or something similar. Therefore I should also reiterate that growth happens when you want it to, and I've grown so much since those days (and I owe those ladies some margaritas!).

The other problem is that negativity tends to hit our emotional core harder than positivity. If somebody says or does something we consider negative, we feel it. We're all human, and we all want to be loved and respected. If somebody doesn't provide us with that kind of validation, we instantly wonder what we need to change about ourselves.

I went through this earlier this year with the payment processing issue I discussed in a previous chapter. Random accounts were being banned or frozen, and one person in particular within my industry was very outspoken about pinning the blame on me.

I had to take a moment when this happened and think about what this meant. Clearly, I'm making an impact in my industry. If I'm in a broad enough space that there are people who love *and* hate me, I've made a splash. As Oscar Wilde once said, "There is only one thing worse than being talked about, and that is not being talked about." If I was flying under the radar and not attracting that kind of attention, I would question whether I was really achieving what I had set out to do. The fact is, if everybody was claiming they loved me, that wouldn't be real.

In addition, I realized that I don't need to respond to these accusations. That's the reclaiming of power and control that I talked about earlier. I remember one night I was scrolling through Instagram, looking for something to take my mind off work, and I saw a post that said, "A lion does not concern themselves with the opinions of sheep." That really struck a chord with me.

Look, some people don't like me. That's fine. I'm not everybody's cup of tea. When they try to blame me for things that have nothing to do with me though? That's just giving me more power. I'll take that all day long! Sometimes you need to detach your own ego and get on with the job at hand. I'd rather be equally loved and loathed by thousands than unstintingly adored by dozens.

Live Your Best Life with a Smile

Maybe the fact that I was born and raised in the United States, with American values, has something to do with my positivity. As a country, we have a very confident culture. In fact, we sometimes have too many people patting themselves on the back for all the wrong reasons!

Overall, though, we're living in an age where people are permitted to love themselves, and I'm onboard with that. I've said it before, and I'll do so again. I firmly believe that self-encouragement is an inside job. Whenever I'm on my morning run, I feel invincible—because I tell myself I am. Just the other morning I was on the beach, about five miles in, and I thought to myself, "Laura, you are killing this. You're on mile five, you're feeling good—go you!"

Right about that time, another girl came running past me. Now, when I say running past me, I mean she left me choking on her dust! She must have been going at least three minutes per mile faster than me. My instant reaction—other than, "Holy crap, that was fast"—was to doubt myself.

I thought I was doing so well, and then the Roadrunner zipped past me. I caught myself pretty quickly though. I realized that I *was* doing well. I had gotten up and out of bed at 5:00 a.m., I was on mile five, I wasn't feeling any ill effects—I was happy with what I had achieved.

Just because somebody else was out there, and it looked like they were doing better than me, it didn't denigrate my own accomplishments. We have to stop that side-by-side comparison. For a start, this other girl was at least fifteen years younger than me. And, hey, for all I know, she was doing a two-mile sprint rather than a longer run.

I was doing what *I* needed to do before my working day. I was cool. She was cool. We were both out there, doing what we had to do. I could have been sitting on my couch drinking my coffee, and in many respects I would have preferred that to covering five miles on a hot, humid beach. That wasn't my goal that morning though.

Sometimes, we meet our goals in the most unexpected ways too. As I've gained more experience in life and work, I've grown better at picking my battles. Sometimes, walking away means that you live to fight another day. I try not to close off opportunity, though, because a solution to problem *A* sometimes occurs while you're wrestling with problem *Z*.

A few years ago, I acquired a company as a personal venture. After the sale went through, I realized that it was very far from what had been presented to me. I did my due diligence, but certain facts had been kept from me. On paper, I could have gone straight into litigation and gotten my money back. I had a watertight case. Unfortunately, I had my hands so full with JVZoo that I just didn't have the capacity. There are only so many hours in a day, and I had to pick my priorities.

That doesn't mean that I wasn't as mad as you know what though. I had been sold a Ferrari, and when I popped the hood, I found that it had the engine of a Toyota. I might have been OK with that if I'd been told up front. Even if I wasn't, somebody else probably would have been interested if they knew what they were dealing with. I was seriously ticked off at the dishonesty of the person that sold me the company. Eventually, I told myself to accept the loss and walk away. I had other fish to fry.

A few weeks later, I had all but forgotten about it. Like I said, I had a whole lot going on at that point. With distance and the cold light of day, I realized exactly what I could do. I could break that company down and sell it in pieces to a variety of different people, all of whom needed exactly what it had to offer. You don't sell a Ferrari with the engine of a Toyota to a collector of sports cars. You find two separate buyers; one who needs the body of a Ferrari and one who needs the engine of a Toyota.

The best thing is that, in doing so, I made my money back almost immediately—and more, I actually turned a profit, after buying a lame duck of a company. That was the ultimate FU to the jerk that screwed me over. They say that living well is the best revenge. When I think back to how much more money that guy could have made if he was just up-front with me, I'm inclined to agree.

Chapter Nine

And Speaking of Sh** . . .

L et's talk about men some more!

Of course, I'm being flippant when I say that. I have said this before, but I'll repeat myself once more for those in the cheap seats—*I do not hate men.* I hate jerks, liars, and people who demean others in pursuit of their own goals, sure. Sadly, as we'll discuss throughout this chapter, those characteristics are not gender-specific.

In fact, I'm going to go one further. I actually *envy* men, in some respects. Not in the Freudian sense. I just think the opposing considerations men and women need to make before even starting their working day, and get wistful. You'll often find me ruminating on the small but consequential differences I'd experience if my name were Lance or Lawrence Casselman.

A Day in the Life

From the moment I wake up in the morning, I'm thinking about work. That's normal—most of us are in the same boat. I can't even *begin* to imagine what it would be like to be in the shower and not think about what I have to do when I reach the office though. That's a privilege that simply isn't available to women in the corporate world. We need to stop and consider *everything*.

Let's take workplace attire as an example. I've talked before about the considerations I need to give to my clothes when I'm in a professional setting. This has always been the case—most notably back when I worked in an office environment in NYC.

I always had to consider what clothing would make me attractive enough to get my foot in the door. However, I also had to ensure that my outfit wouldn't be declared slutty, or have me written off as stupid before I even opened my mouth. If somebody was just going to stare at my legs for an hour and not listen to a word I said, I was wasting my time.

This is a constant balancing act for women. Even today, walk through a major city and you'll see women with "to and from shoes." They'll have shoes that are comfortable and practical enough to negotiate the subway or a busy street, and then heels for the office that provide the appropriate aesthetic.

Now, I have railed against this by introducing a different culture in my company. I don't care what my team wears in the office (within reason). Sometimes, I wear my workout clothes to work if I plan to squeeze in a run or a trip to the gym during the day. That's part of the fun of getting to set the rules.

These considerations have never really impacted men in the workplace though. They put on a suit, and maybe their toughest decision is which color tie matches their shirt best. Now, I'm not belittling the fact that men need to wear suits in the blistering heat.

Taking public transport dressed that way is horrific, and I'd never deny that. Having said that, I'd wager that men have never had other men run their hands down the back of their legs in a crowded subway train either. That particular delight is reserved for women in skirts—and I speak from personal experience. All I could do was throw an elbow and fight my way off the train at the next stop.

Once they get to work, suit untouched by the wandering hands of opportunistic strangers, men can get on with the task at hand. They don't need to worry about whether the women they will do business with are casting a verdict about them and their competence based on their suit. For women, the judgment is only just beginning at this point.

As we established back in Chapter 5, I curse like a sailor that tossed his swear jar overboard. Based on my upbringing, I'm supposed to act like a lady and use language to match that stereotype. As you know, I say, "F that." I *am* a lady, and I'm a woman that has earned the right to sit at the big boy's table.

I still feel the need to moderate my language in that setting though. Men can turn the air blue and earn a pat on the back and a hearty chuckle for their trouble. When a woman drops an F-bomb at work, there aren't enough pearl necklaces and fainting couches to go around. If she's wearing red while she does so? Forget about it—she's branded a raging witch with a b incapable of controlling her emotions.

These are just tiny drops in the ocean when I consider the difference between male and female experiences in the workplace. Before I've even finished my first cup of coffee, I have mentally run through countless gauntlets and negotiated a lot of potential pitfalls. The opportunity to just turn up at work and do my job? That's an impossible dream for me, and every other woman out there.

Not Bad . . . for a Girl

I was recently at an overseas industry event where I gave a pretty big speech. It was important to me, so when I was done I asked an audience member I trusted how he thought it went.

He told me it went well—but then explained that a number of men in the audience felt compelled to tell him, "Yeah, yeah, great speech and all—I had no idea she was so pretty though." Great, so these chuckleheads hadn't listened to a word I said while I was on stage. That was worth an eight thousand-mile round trip.

Later that night, I went to a dinner for the speakers and attendees of the event that had bought VIP tickets. At these events, there's *always* a guy that tries to bring me down a level. This one was no exception. Maybe he was acting subconsciously and didn't realize he was doing it. I'm probably giving him too much credit, though, and ascribing layers he doesn't possess.

Anyway, our friend came up with one of my least favorite assessments of my character. "Oh, you're nothing like you come across online!" he gleefully informed me. "You're actually super-cute in person."

OK, friend, I'm going to stop you there. Don't call me "cute"—because I'm not. Puppies are cute. Baby shoes are cute. Successful women in business are not "cute." We are intelligent and driven, and that makes certain people uncomfortable. That's why people like this guy need to try to bring us down a level, so they find it easier to engage and retain some misapprehension of power.

In such situations, I have to remind myself that even if I did drop a level—or two, or three—I'd still outrank this guy. I am the CEO of an international company, and he is . . . well, let's just say he is not. We were not even close to being equals in job title or salary. I want to say to people something like this, "You may be bringing me down a peg in your head, but perception is not reality."

These days, I don't need to say that. I don't even need to react. I'll take another sip of my drink and look for somebody more worthy of my time to talk to. I remember this happening so much while I climbed the ladder though. The men would be addressed by name, but I was always, "Blondie." It's little things like this that are designed to bring women down.

Nowadays, in the real game of life and business, I'm above these people. It doesn't bother me. When we were supposed to be equals, though, it *did*. There are countless women going through this right now. This needs to change. It's not cool to address Joe, Tom, and Pat as Joe, Tom, and Pat, but to demean Christina, Jennifer, and Laura by calling them Cutie, Honey, and Blondie.

Sisters Doing It for Themselves

I give a firm handshake. A normal, firm handshake. That's something I learned very early in my career. I look somebody in the eye and shake their hand, making it clear from the get-go that I'm here to do business. If somebody holds out a kind of paw, as though they want to clasp my dainty little digits in their hand? I have no patience for that.

I bring this up because men seem surprised by that. I think maybe they expect me to curtsey. I can immediately tell how a man feels about doing business with me by their reaction to a firm handshake and eye contact. If they back up and start saying, "Whoa there, no need to be so forceful!" I know I'm in for a long afternoon. This is yet another double standard among genders.

Misconceptions about women in business still abound too. Believe it not, we have no interest in spending ten minutes discussing whether or not we think our cat may have OCD. From my experience, women are more forthright and just want to get business done. All the same, they can be tougher nuts to crack—especially for a fellow female.

Whenever I attend a conference, there are two things I know I need to do. I need to find and talk to the person who organized the event, and I need to seek out the women. The longer you wait to approach a high-ranking woman, the more she'll quietly judge you from afar.

This isn't always easy. Sometimes the women at these events avoid me. They know my position, and they're either nervous about engaging with me, or they want to know if I consider myself too important to speak to them. I'll still track these women down though. I want them to know I am friendly and do not place myself on any kind of pedestal. I'll find them, say hello, explain that I need to go and discuss something elsewhere, but make it clear that I have seen them and will look to reconnect later.

As I've said before, when I worked in sales in New York, male clients were easy. Some of them found me attractive, and if that got me past the gatekeeper, then fine. I've also said before that the game is stupid, but I wasn't the umpire back then. I couldn't change the rules. I just had to do whatever I could within them.

Women, though, were much tougher. I've discussed my own experiences in this book, and as you'll see, it's rarely an easy ride. This was ten or fifteen years ago, though, when things were even harder. These women would have worked their absolute butts off to get where they were. I've been through crap, but even I can't imagine what the women then experienced to reach positions of seniority.

Naturally, this has consequences. They were not polite, and they were not nice to me. There was no sisterhood, no sense that it was good to see a woman climbing the ladder. They were just abrasive and cold. I vowed that this wasn't how I wanted to be when I achieved my own goals. It almost felt like they were punishing me for their male colleagues deeming me attractive. Maybe they were. I later discovered that men place a great deal of emphasis on aesthetics.

Is Everything OK at Home, Laura?

Once upon a time, I dyed my hair dark brown. Let's make one thing clear—it did not go well. It looked so bad that my father told me not to come home until I had changed it back. I'm joking, but not really! This experience taught me a few things. Mainly that I am not equipped to be a brunette. The experiment also had a knock-on effect though.

When I first moved to NYC, I wondered why people wouldn't hold doors open for me. I grew up in the South, where that's an automatic action. It took me a while to learn how to make eye contact while approaching a door, as though to say, "Wait for me please." After I dyed my hair, even that didn't work. Men simply would not hold the door for me. That's not because brown hair doesn't get you what blonde hair does. It's because brown hair looked *really bad* on me.

The flipside to this was I was taken much more seriously in business. Women were nicer to me, and men actually listened to what I had to say. They had no interest in me physically, so, hey, maybe I had something relevant to share.

This is the life of the woman in the workplace. We have to be attractive, but not so attractive that we're deemed a distraction to the men in the building. We have to be smart, but not so smart that we intimidate our poor, delicate male counterparts. And we certainly can't react to situations the same way a man does.

If a man is hosting a meeting, he can break to crack a joke, and everybody will laugh. The moment he returns to business, people will immediately step back in line. That just doesn't happen with women. If a woman makes a joke, it seems to suck all the air out of the room. Men in the room start huffing and puffing, demanding to know if we're all here to do business or if we're clowning around. It's as exhausting as it is frustrating.

If a male CEO holds a meeting and says, "These numbers are crap—what's going on?" people will fall over themselves to apologize and offer an explanation. If a woman takes the same line, the response is more likely to be, "You can't speak to us that way! Are you feeling OK? Is something wrong at home?"

Imagine how much I *love* that.

I'll make something clear before we go any further. It's not just men who are guilty of this reaction. I experienced this last year courtesy of a woman in another company.

This woman—let's call her Karen—was an account manager. I held that position about twelve years ago, and I worked really hard to get from there to where I am now. I don't care that her company is bigger than mine. I worked for a firm of equal size when I had her job title.

I was on a call to this company, and I was in the process of chewing them out about something extremely important that they had repeatedly messed up. The response was, "Well, Karen *did* say you might be a little upset right now because your father is sick. Maybe you're taking out your sadness on the people you work with?"

Fun fact—I was actually upset because my company had lost $21 million thanks to Karen and her cohorts not doing their jobs properly. You have cost my business *$21 million dollars*, and you want to bring up my personal life? Grow up, Karen.

I *wanted* to say that was why Karen would only ever be an account manager. I *wanted* to repeat all the condescending crap I have been subjected to in my career, up to and including asking Karen if she was just being a witch with a b because she was on her period. Weeks of delays had turned into months of delays, and they still didn't have any answers for me. My company was still hemorrhaging money because they couldn't get their sh** together. And yet, the only *possible* reason I was being aggressive and demanding action on this call was because my father was ill?

You won't be surprised to know that Karen is no longer my account manager. She is no longer on my list of people to care about. I don't have time for anybody who's incapable of putting their big girl pants on and coming to work. I certainly don't have time for people who use those kinds of deflection tactics to cover for their own inadequacies.

Earn Your Opportunities

I have given the younger generation a tough time in this book so far. As much as they frustrate me with their desire to bring frou-frou, happy-clappy feelings into the workplace, I'll say something for young people in business. They are far less likely to question a female in authority. This warms my heart a little. It seems that, slowly but surely, we're no longer being seen as an anomaly.

It's the people my age, and the generation above, who are the condescending types. That's my issue with people like Karen. She and I are around the same age.

I don't doubt she's ticked off that she hasn't got past the account manager stage of her career. I know I was keen to leave the role in my dust as soon as I could. Her behavior makes her part of the problem though. She didn't show a backbone when she needed to, and if you don't stand against something that contradicts your values, then you are compliant in it. In Karen's case, I'm sure she's been belittled at work because she's a woman. This is why it got me so worked up that she took such a personal angle with me.

I get that standing up for yourself can be a tricky minefield to negotiate. Not everybody can plant their flag on day one—there is a hierarchy in the corporate world, whether you agree with it or not. As we've discussed before, you need to pay your dues in life.

Paying your dues doesn't mean accepting less than you deserve, though—and it certainly doesn't mean that you should try to drag somebody else down instead of pulling yourself up. Read that again. Seriously. If the option is to drag others down or pull yourself up, rise! Dig your fingernails in, grit your teeth, and pull yourself up!

I'm a firm believer in grasping opportunities as and when they arise. Opportunity and equality are often linked though. Take education as an example. Somebody who went to an Ivy League college will typically find themselves with more opportunities than somebody with a community college degree. As a result, they'll typically earn more money.

Personally, I don't care what school you went to. I want to know what you've *achieved*. Ivy League schools don't have a magic arch that automatically bestows an additional fifty IQ points upon anybody who walks beneath it. Somebody else may be just as smart but attended community college for any number of reasons.

The same applies to reputation too. If Mr. Montgomery IV wants to stand up in a meeting and declare that we should do things a certain way, I'll listen. If he has bad ideas, I'll tell him—I don't care if that upsets people. Good on you for coming from a famous and successful family, Mr. Montgomery IV. Bravo on being born. Until you show me that you can match your family name with good ideas, it means nothing to me. Are we doing business or not? Kissing booty isn't my style.

The Return of the Prodigal Son

Another thing I have noticed is that a man who has been out of the business for a prolonged period can step back whenever he wants. Want to take a year out of the game to sit on the sidelines? That's fine. Just put that suit back on when you're ready, and people will be happy to hang on your every word.

Here's the thing though: while our man was MIA, sitting on those sidelines, I was still *in* the game. I was observing the changes to the rules. I was kicking the winning field goal. And yet, when I point out that things have changed and his suggestions won't fly in the current climate, *I'm* the one who gets questioned.

Well, sure, that makes sense. I mean, this guy has been on his couch polishing his bowling trophies for the last year while I was running a company, but let's assume that he knows better.

Sometimes, I'll let people run with this and tell my team to try it this way. I'll let that test run for as long as I can afford to allow it. Some tests can only run a couple of days before the hit to revenue becomes too great. Some can run for closer to a month. Eventually, either way, the lesson is learned.

I find this so baffling. Again, it's not just male employees who follow a returning man blindly. Women do it too. I have to remind them that I'm fighting so hard for equality, and yet every time a man opens his mouth, they act as though it's a sacred gospel. It's almost as though it's ingrained in them that the man is always right. I have a problem with that. Guess what, kids? Sometimes, the man is an idiot.

Life moves quickly in our world. What worked yesterday will usually be obsolete by tomorrow. I don't have the time or inclination to pick up the pieces when people forget this.

> **When you take time away from the game, it doesn't mean you can't come back and catch up, but if you haven't been in the field, it's best not to act like you have.**

Show some respect to those who remained in the arena while you stepped away. Get caught up, get back in the game, and then play to win!

Insights from the Outside

Maybe this is a universal trait. Men at other companies sometimes approach me and ask me to work with them because they've seen that I get results. I always explain that I can't take on a full-time role, but I'll work with them on a consultancy basis.

I'll also make a few things clear right from the start. I'll make sure they understand that I'm direct. For some reason, that quality in a woman upsets people. I'll tell them that I'm going to cut straight to the core of their business and tell them where their problems are. If it's a personnel issue, I won't beat around the bush—I'll tell them where the dead weight is and that they need to get rid of certain people if they want to see results. Finally, I'll make it obvious that I expect them to listen to my advice. It's what they're paying me for.

Invariably, we end up having the same conversation two or three months in a row, and I have to pull them up on it. They're repeating the same behavior, despite the advice that I have provided, and asking the same questions at particular points in the month. I will always give them the same answer, and eventually I'll tell them that I'm going to ignore that question in the future. I have given them the answer they need, and I've repeated myself because they're paying me to do so. There are limits to my patience though.

It's interesting, because their instinct will always be to become defensive and say that isn't happening. Fast-forward to that same point the following month, though, and they'll catch themselves and say, "Oh. You said this would happen."

As a consultant, I'll tell somebody something twice. That's once more than I do in my own company! If they're paying me enough, I'll tell them three times. After that, I'm wasting my time. I'm just a record that's spinning on repeat, and everybody stopped listening a long time ago.

Some people may be OK with just continually taking somebody's money if they're not prepared to do what is necessary. I'm not. I care about my reputation for efficiency. If getting involved with another business means that I risk my reputation taking a hit, I'll wrap up that relationship and move on. This is so important.

I once met with a marketing company, and I thought the meeting went well. My suspicions were confirmed when I got a letter from the president of the company saying he really enjoyed the meeting and considered it one of the best he'd ever had. However, he had done some research and decided he wasn't going to work with us. He told me that he'd be delighted to work with me on a personal level, but he was at a point where he didn't tie in his fortunes with companies he did not want to work with.

As you can probably imagine, I was curious. I got in touch and thanked him for taking the time to write to me personally rather than just sending out a form letter, and asked if we could meet to discuss what went wrong. I'm always learning, and I'm the leader of this company. I was sure there was something I could take from the conversation.

We met for coffee, and I have to say, I admire this guy a lot. He had built a great business based on defining hard lines about whom he wanted to work with. He explained *why* he had decided not to forge a relationship with my company, and I totally understood and respected his decision. Ever since then, I have taken a leaf out of his book when it comes to performing due diligence.

Any time I am looking into a potential collaboration, I do serious background checks. Business is one thing, but if I'm going to partner up with somebody? I need to know about the *character* of the person I'm working with, not just their financial acumen. We don't need to be friends, but I do need you not to be a complete jerk with values that contradict mine.

If I'm looking at a partnership and I discover that it's with a man that hits his wife, for example, that's not somebody I'm hitching my wagon to. Frankly, that's for his safety, not mine. I don't trust myself not to throw a right hook and show him how it feels to be on the receiving end.

In addition, I'll reiterate what I said back in Chapter 7. Anybody entering into a business partnership should plan the eventual divorce at the same time as the wedding. Not every collaboration lasts forever. In fact, most don't. Just like in a marriage, you may start to want different things over time, and it's tough to compromise and reconcile those varying wishes.

Plan out what will happen with *every* asset if and when the time comes that you no longer wish to work together. There does not need to be recriminations and lawsuits. The trouble is, if the relationship breaks down, *everybody* wants *everything*. Just like married couples fight over custody of the family dog, business partners start to squabble over staplers and coffee pots.

The moment attorneys get involved, communication stops, and a fight begins. Nobody wants to concede ground, and it just becomes increasingly bitter. If you take the right action in advance, you can professionally part ways having both obtained everything you wanted from the partnership.

You also need to think about the equality of your workload. If you're a marketer, you may have a great idea. You'll need a developer to bring the project to life before you market it though. Neither of you are experts in running a business, so you bring in a third person to handle that. Great. You're now a trinity, all of whom have equal shares in the business.

Think about the longer-term implications of this. Maybe the developer only has to work on the project in the beginning, and then he's done. Alternatively, maybe he has a constant job of updating and improving the product. Maybe you only need to run one marketing campaign at launch before you sit back and count your money. It's more likely that you'll constantly be running new promotions to drum up interest though.

People say they don't care about sharing money in the beginning. They're just excited to get the project off the ground. What if it makes a million dollars? A third of that money isn't to be sneezed at. What happens if it makes another million a month later though? Another million the month after that? How are you going to divide up that pay?

This might sound like a first-world problem. Many people will say they'd cut off their own pinky for $333,333 a month. Ask yourself a question though. How would you feel if you were working eighty-hour weeks for that money while somebody else was taking an equal share while working eight hours a month? Or better yet, how would you feel if you knew that you all could be tripling your income if the other put his full forty hours a week in rather a lousy two.

You'll feel like your pocket is being picked, and you're going to get angry. It doesn't matter that you were broke when you started and now you have a million dollars. In that situation, you're going to feel like you should have three million. That's going to sting. Rightfully so.

Everybody Wants to Rule the World

I haven't been very complimentary about men in business throughout this chapter, so I'll turn the tables a little. Let's picture a world that has been flipped on its axis, and women hold the majority of senior positions in the workplace. Would it *really* be that different?

In truth, probably not. It would be great karma, but I think if the roles were reversed, it would be equally as bad. I feel that more people need to realize that while we're on the right track, we're still too far from implementing real change across the board. Globally, women are still two hundred-ish years away from equal pay. That is crazy to me.

There is still so much to do, and it starts with leadership. I recently saw a social media post that asked how many people were aware that women are not paid equally, and I can't tell you how many men commented. You can probably imagine what was said. Apparently, this is a fictional claim and it's been blown out of all proportion.

Once I'd finished swearing, I decided to combat opinions with facts. What people forget is that while women are starting to receive equal pay in some countries, we *are* still being bypassed for promotions that we're eminently qualified for in favor of men.

OK, maybe that happened to a man too. Once. We're likely looking at around one incident in a hundred.

Now, before anybody starts throwing the pregnancy argument at me, let's take another fact into consideration. There are more women having babies in this decade than the last. That's because ten years ago, women had to put families on hold to stand any chance of getting a job in the STEM fields. This is also why women are having babies so much later in life.

If women in positions of authority *do* have children, they rarely return to work. This isn't because their brains have turned to mush, and they'd much rather be singing nursery rhymes and looking at local schools than working. I'd wager that most of these women value changing the world every bit as highly as they do changing diapers.

It's because companies don't provide help with childcare and don't take these personal circumstances into consideration. These are policies that are primarily devised by men, lest we forget. It means that most women are running up huge expenses to find somebody to watch their children, in addition to being responsible for 75 percent of what people call "invisible work" around the home.

Women do the majority of household chores, and they take care of the kids and any elderly parents. Sorry, men, if you're the exception to the rule, then all power to you, but it's true. After a day at work, women are expected to cook dinner, bathe the kids, and check in on their parents. Most men may work longer hours, but they get to return home when this is complete. They may read the kids a bedtime story and kiss them goodnight, but the heavy lifting has been done.

Like I said, I realize that this is not universal. There are amazing men out there doing amazing things. Overall, though, this is a huge problem. Personally, I took only a few days off for maternity leave, and I did not do so willingly. I had some complications with the birth of my daughter, and due to the medications given to me in the hospital, I was unable to work the full time I was in labor. As I type this, I think how insane it is to have planned to have worked during my labor, but I did. And mostly I did this because I was worried about the clients I consult with. But that's how high-level women are conditioned. We are so accustomed to doing twice, three, or four times the amount of work of our male counterparts to be considered equal.

So when talking about "invisible work" in the home, consider, do you leave your damp towel on the floor for your partner to pick up, do you put your socks in the laundry basket or drop them carelessly on the floor, or do you fail to close the pantry door? It's ten seconds here and ten seconds there, but it all adds up. Throw kids into the mix, too, and that *really* adds up. Is your partner or wife asking you to do the same simple things around the house and then reminding you a month later, and again a month after that?

So when I see men making comments about how pay inequality is an imaginary media narrative, it gets under my skin. It's something that I feel passionate about. It's something that I lived through, and it's something I see women that I deeply respect live through every day. Women that enable this attitude are part of the problem. If you want to say that women just need to work harder and that I'm only getting hot about this because my dad is sick, that's your business. I'll repeat my party line on that though. Go *F* yourself, Karen.

Chapter Ten

Know Your Value

When you're weighed down by the invisible work that we discussed in the previous chapter, it can be difficult to find time for yourself. In fact, women in particular often mistakenly believe that carving out time for ourselves to meet our own physical and emotional needs is somehow selfish.

This could not be further from the truth. If you're not taking care of yourself, you'll be in no condition to take care of anybody else. It's like the sign on an airplane says—in the event of an emergency, fasten your own oxygen mask before you help somebody else with theirs.

Recognizing this and taking time out for yourself is an essential part of knowing and understanding your own value. Unfortunately, you'll encounter a whole lot of people in this world who do not acknowledge your value. In fact, they may even attempt to strip it from you.

I've shared enough of my own experiences in previous chapters to show you that this doesn't stop once you reach a certain position of seniority. In fact, if anything, it just makes you a potentially more impressive wall display for an aspiring trophy hunter.

There is good news, though; nobody can take away your value but *you*. By standing firm and carving out the time you need, you can ensure that you stand tall and proud and are the best version of yourself possible. That is the best possible revenge you can enact on anybody who tries to bring you down.

The Struggle Is Real

I know firsthand how hard it can be to find the balance between meeting your commitments and retaining a sense of self. I have talked before about how important exercise and eating well is to me. That stems from my time as a dancer. I had regular weigh-ins, and I always had to keep one eye on my weight. I had no problem with doing so, though, because I was acutely aware that I also felt great when I was in shape.

For the longest time, I walked the two worlds of corporate America and dance gigs. I may have a head for business, but I also have the heart and soul of a performer. I never wanted to step out of the dance world and start again at the ground level, and thankfully, I didn't need to. I made sure I was in dancing condition, in case an opportunity arose at short notice.

While I was the COO of JVZoo, I managed to balance those commitments. I was working long hours, but I was still managing to work out regularly. I felt great, and I knew I was doing a good job. The world was my oyster. Then I took on the CEO position, and it was a whole new ball game.

I went from working long hours to working *insane* hours. This was partly because the job demanded it—you won't find many

CEOs that work an eight-hour day—but also because of the expectations I placed upon myself. I wanted to be great, and I wouldn't settle for anything less.

I wasn't the first new CEO of JVZoo since Bryan Zimmerman, the co-founder of the company, stepped down from the role. I was the first new CEO that was announced to the public though. This meant that I was very much under scrutiny within the industry. I wanted to do great things, and I was determined to build the best possible service platform for our users.

Before I knew it, a couple of months had passed in what felt like the blink of an eye. I was in my late thirties at this point, and for the first time in my life, I hadn't been able to find the time to work out and take care of myself in that way. I had to sit down and think about how I was going to fit everything in.

Like I said before, taking care of ourselves is *not* selfish. The human body isn't like a car. We only have one, and if it breaks down, we can't just pick up a new and improved model. This isn't a vanity thing either; all kinds of positive things happen when you work out. Endorphins are released, and you feel much happier, and that's by design. We're supposed to *realize* that exercise is a good thing!

All the same, it took me a while to permit myself the time to work out. I had to convince myself that taking this time for myself wasn't just OK—it was *essential*. I started reading about and studying the great leaders and innovative thinkers of our world, and it became increasingly obvious that they all made their health a priority.

Taking care of our body helps us take care of our mind. Dave Asprey, who wrote the book *Game Changers: What Leaders, Innovators, and Mavericks Do to Win at Life*, talks a lot about bio-hacking to make himself as smart as he can be. He even talks about micro-dosing LSD, which a lot of people have done. In case my grandmother is reading this, I'd like to make it abundantly clear that I have not!

There's so much we can do to make ourselves more attentive throughout the day though. That was the whole basis behind Bulletproof Coffee—which, in case you're not aware, is filter coffee mixed with butter and coconut oil. That may not sound appealing if you're not on a ketogenic or other high-fat, low-carb diet, but it's another way that we can keep our brains on chart through a long and trying day.

There's more to taking care of ourselves than just physical exercise too. Some people place a great deal of value on meditation and mindfulness. Just taking a moment to allow your brain to have a little time off is so important. If we don't, decision fatigue becomes increasingly likely.

You Choose, I Don't Mind. No, You're Choosing Wrong!

Decision fatigue is a real thing. It's not unique to CEOs, either—parents experience it too. When you spend your entire day answering questions and making decisions, there comes a time that you run out of steam and say, "Whatever, do what you want." That's typically when things start to go south!

I experienced decision fatigue before I knew what it was. It was usually around the time that I had to choose what to eat for dinner. Women have a bad reputation for this. How many times have you had this conversation with your partner?

"What do you want to eat tonight?"

"Anything. I don't mind."

"Are you sure?"

"Yes, honestly. I'm hungry, and I'm so tired that I don't care. Put something in front of me and I'll eat it."

"OK, I'll book a table at that Italian restaurant downtown."

"Ugh, no. I don't want Italian."

We know what we *don't* want, but making a decision about what we *do* becomes impossible when you've been thinking on your feet for fourteen hours straight. I used to drive around aimlessly, passing hundreds of different restaurants, because the idea of actually making a choice was too exhausting. I was just prolonging the inevitable, and it was no way to live.

That can be prevented. There are so many tricks you can use. Don't read your emails first thing in the morning. That's just piling a whole load of new questions on your plate before you've even finished your coffee. Don't check social media first thing either. In my business, what's happening on Facebook has a huge impact on my industry. It's not my job to look at our company's Facebook page though—that's why I hire somebody else to do it. By checking those messages myself, I'm diminishing that employee's value. If something needs my attention, it will be escalated to me.

> Keep your head clear until you've made all of your major decisions for the day ahead—or at least as many of them as possible. If you're not careful, a hundred small decisions will use up all of your brainpower before you manage to make a handful of big ones. It's like death by a thousand cuts.

Thankfully, I understood decision fatigue and had solid tools in place for best managing this before I had my daughter. I can't imagine how I would have been able to handle making the best decisions for her well-being and the businesses I run if I did not have a plan in place for prioritizing what needs my attention first and what I can delegate to others.

Manage Your Ego

Of course, we also need to be careful not to take a wicked sense of pride from pushing beyond our physical and mental limits. Work can sometimes be addictive, especially when you're making a real difference. In some respects, doing a job releases a different set of endorphins. Ego kicks in at this point.

Part of taking care of yourself is keeping your ego in check. Your ego does not have your best interests in mind. We all have things that we prioritize because they're important to us, and we feel like we have to punish ourselves for success. It's a thought process of, "I wanted the big job title, I wanted the office with a view, I've made my bed, and now I have to lie in it. All of this could be taken away at a moment's notice if I don't."

Guess what—you don't. Yes, you need to sustain your performance, but worrying about things that may or not may not happen will not prevent them from happening. You have that job title and that office because you *earned* it. Past tense.

That's why I was given the title of CEO. My name wasn't drawn from a lottery because the previous CEO was tired of the job and needed a quick replacement. That's not what companies that make a lot of money do. They look for the right person, and they think long and hard before making an offer. I earned the title of CEO through my performance as COO of JVZoo for a number of years, and I earned *that* opportunity through my performance at my previous jobs.

Now, when I took the CEO job, I definitely had concerns. I was wondering if people would think, "Who is this (whisper it quietly) *female* taking up such a senior role in our industry?" Even though I had spent quite some time as COO, I was still known as "Laura from Support." I fixed problems that came through the support department, but the head of support reported to me. Even when I was announced as CEO, people would say, "Laura is great at support. She's ideal for this role."

That's not how the trajectory in business works. That's missing a huge number of steps. You can't become a CEO because you're good at answering support tickets any more than you can headline a Hollywood movie because you put in one good performance in your fifth-grade school play. There's nothing to say that you can't get there in the future, but right now, there is more work to be done and a whole lot more to learn.

This played into my concern that, as a woman, I wouldn't be taken seriously in the role. That I would automatically be written off as inferior to my male predecessor, despite everything I had done in my capacity as COO, such as increasing revenue and building the company. In addition, what nobody else knew was that I had already been running the company for a year. I still had the COO job title, but I was handed CEO responsibilities. That was my test—to see if I was up to the job, and if I even wanted it.

So I had the reins of the company for a year, when it was at its biggest. I couldn't take the credit for this, though, because it had not been announced. Then somebody lied about me publicly—and a huge number of people in the industry believed it, without a second thought. Nobody stopped to look at my track record. Nobody stopped to think, "That's weird, she's always been so helpful and friendly with me, and she's clearly smart."

It was exactly what I had feared. Somebody had lied about me, and suddenly all my achievements and hours spent sacrificing sleep and grinding myself to the bone did nothing to stop it. Ultimately, some people are still stuck in the dark ages. They just cannot fathom or comprehend that little ol' Laura from Support could possibly be smart enough to pull all these achievements off.

With the benefit of hindsight, I should have spent my time formulating a plan about how I would react when this happened. As it was, I wasted months worrying about it—and there was nothing I could do to prevent it from unfolding. It was a lesson learned, but I wish I could have gained that wisdom without sacrificing my health.

Take Stock Before It's Too Late

On Sundays or public holidays, I work what I call a half day—I typically work around six or seven hours. Now, for most people, a full working day is eight hours, and that would be between Monday and Friday. Back when I first started as a CEO, I felt like I was cheating by taking even this time to myself.

When you're a CEO, you never really have a full day away. It's like being a parent. There's my actual child, and then my second child, the company. If you're a parent and your kid needs something, you're up—you can't wave that away and expect somebody else to pick up the slack. It's the same in my role. A big part of the gig is stepping up and taking responsibility when the crap hits the fan.

Sometimes, though, you need to take as close to a full day away as you can. If you don't, your brain turns to mush, and you lose the ability to make good decisions and have innovative ideas. You're just on the hamster wheel, going through the motions.

It took a tragedy for me to finally tear myself away from work for anything resembling a prolonged period. I got a phone call at lunch one day, informing me that my dad had been taken into the hospital for a routine check-up, and they were not allowing him to leave. I wasn't worried at this point. I thought it would all turn out OK. I told my team that I just had to get my mom through the next hour or so at the hospital, and then I'd be back. I was only a phone call away on my cell if they needed me.

I got to the hospital five minutes before a doctor emerged and announced that they had a real mess on their hands. They were talking about needing to perform six heart bypasses. Thankfully, it ended up "only" being a quadruple bypass. Following that, however, he had a heart attack and then a stroke.

It took this horrible situation for me to realize just what had been happening to me. For the past two years I hadn't just lost sight of taking care of myself; I had lost sight of how important it was to me to be a good daughter, which is a value that I treasure above just about anything else. We talked back in Chapter 5 about the importance of learning what you give an *F* about, and I give a whole bunch of *F*s about my family. They're the most important thing in the world to me. Somewhere along the line, the lines between work and life had become too blurred for comfort, and something had to change.

I'm not saying that being a good CEO and being a good daughter are mutually exclusive. You can definitely be both. There just has to be a cut-off time when work ends and life begins. That's another critical element of knowing your value. Just because you got that job title and that fancy office, it doesn't mean you get to check out from being a human being.

Nowadays, I make sure I take a break in the afternoon to call my family and check in. Sometimes it's just a five-minute call. Sometimes it's thirty minutes. The important thing is that I do this, instead of just grinding away. If I skipped that call, would I have done more at work? Maybe. In truth, though, I typically get that task done anyway, at the same speed as I would have without taking a break. That conversation with my family gives my brain a rest and allows me to reset my mental equilibrium. After that, I'm ready to face the business world all over again.

Before this happened to me, I had a mentality—and I think it's a pretty common one—where I thought, "If I just achieve this *one last thing*, then I can take a step back." That's BS though. When we reach that finish line, it feels great. Naturally, this means we look for the next accomplishment we can target.

I remember the first milestone that I set for myself, earlier in my career. It was a financial target, and I thought that if I reached that salary, I'd be able to take a step back. It makes me laugh now. It was about a quarter of my current salary, and when I see that number written down, I almost gasp. I think, I could never live on that kind of money!

Clearly I can. I did so for a number of years, so I know exactly how to do it! I also have more in my savings now than ever before, because I pay myself from every paycheck before I do anything else. Even then, though, I was looking for the next milestone.

Some people never reach a point where they think they're done. I'm quite sure I'm one of those people. I'm trying to change the world here, and that's an ongoing task. Putting my feet up, mixing a cocktail, and saying, "Call me when the business world is equal," isn't an option for me. I want to be a part of the change. I need to make the playing field more equal for when my daughter is on it. And trust me when I say, I'm just getting started.

Understand Your Parameters

When you work for somebody else, your performance is beholden to their goals. As CEO, I answer to a board of directors. If I can deliver what they're expecting of me—and the company— then I'm doing a good job. If I continue to improve the service we offer our users, I'm doing a good job. Ultimately, the purpose of a business is to solve problems. If I can help my business ride out a storm, and nothing more severe than hammering a few boards and nails back into place in the aftermath is required, then I'm doing a good job.

The important thing is to know exactly what those expectations are before you sign up for a job. If you deliver on those expectations, then you're a valuable employee. Naturally, you'll hope that your employer will recognize that value. The first step is to acknowledge and recognize it yourself though.

Delivering value is so important, for a number of reasons—not the least of which is for your own sake. You'll have your own career and financial milestones that you want to reach at work. Maybe you want to graduate from an internship to an associate position. Maybe you want to take another step up the ladder. Maybe you just want a fair and reasonable raise based on the value you're delivering in your performance.

That's all fine—but only if you *are* delivering. As we have discussed before in this book, the world does not owe you a thing, and life and business are not fair. Always check that the value you are delivering matches up to—or better yet, exceeds—the expectations of the business or person that pays your salary.

Of course, as a female, there is always an extra wrinkle to observe. You need to check that you are being treated the same as your male counterparts. It's unfortunate that we still have to do this, but we do.

If your male colleagues are constantly gaining promotions and pay increases and you're not, you need to look at why. Ask yourself, are you delivering the same performance as them? Are you delivering *better* results than them? If so, sadly this suggests that your value is not being recognized and respected. In these cases, it's time to move on to a new employer who *will* recognize what you have to offer.

If not, the answer is obvious—use their career trajectory as motivation to gain a slice of that pie for yourself. Your stagnation has nothing to do with your gender and everything to do with your performance. You're not meeting the expectations that have been set for you, so why should you be rewarded?

You wouldn't leave a generous tip for a restaurant server who forgot to take your order, poured hot coffee in your lap, and let your food go cold while they chatted with their friends. Your employer takes the same approach. If you're not delivering value to a business, you're a drain on their resources. Why would they be keen to make sure you stick around, if that's the case?

Drawing a Line in the Sand

It's also important to remember the difference between your value as an employee and your value as a human being. There are some lines that I won't cross, as I've discussed before. I've reached a point in my life when I can walk away when anybody tries to cross those lines. I don't care if you're my boss, a shareholder, a coworker, or a customer. I will not stand for certain treatment.

I had an incident recently where one of the women who work on my support desk (she really *does* work on the support desk) showed me some of the vile messages she was getting from customers who were experiencing issues.

Look, I understand being upset. I'll always try to help anybody who retains a calm and cool demeanor and speaks to us with respect. I will not tolerate abuse of my team, though—especially when this employee knows more about the system than anybody else, and she was being patronized as well as insulted. I told her to change her name on the chat to a man's name, and what do you know, the entire tone of the messages changed. Sometimes you have to play the game, but sometimes you just have to walk away and say, "Good luck without me." You absolutely *cannot* let somebody else take your value away from you.

In a perfect world, we'd walk into every situation in our lives with a clear idea of what we'll tolerate and what we won't. It's nice to think that we could say, "If *this* happens, I'll walk away." A boss asking to meet in a hotel lobby and expecting a BJ in exchange for handing over a paycheck, for example.

The fact is, though, sometimes things come up that you're just not expecting—like a boss asking to meet in a hotel lobby and expecting a BJ in exchange for handing over a paycheck! Another example I shared previously, where I was expected to go on a date with a mortgage broker to secure a preferential rate for my boss, falls into the same category.

I never could have predicted that I'd be subjected to these things at work. For anybody who values and respects others, that kind of behavior would not enter your head as a possibility. Now, it's just another story for the collection! If anybody tried to pull the same stunt now, I would politely but firmly inform them that they're off their rocker if they think I'm going to be pimped out as a personal favor. The politeness may get lost in translation somewhere.

If you're placed in a similar situation, never stop questioning how you feel about it. I'm not saying take a month to mull it over from every possible angle though. Sometimes, if you're put in a position that makes you feel instantly uncomfortable, you need to remove yourself from it straight away. Calm down and take a moment to think about it, and decide if you're OK with it after all.

If you're not—as is your right, as nobody should ever be made to feel uncomfortable at work—report it to whoever seems relevant. Maybe that's an HR department, maybe it's your line manager. Either way, you need to know that you raised an issue and that you are valued enough to be taken seriously. If you feel that this isn't the case, you are well within your rights to say that you're not prepared to accept this judgment. If they tell you to accept it or be fired, you still have a choice—you can say, "There's no need to fire me. I quit." If these people do not value you enough to protect you, show them that you value yourself.

I regularly have to remind the female members of my team that we're in a male-dominated industry when we go to events. I always tell them the same thing. If somebody crosses a line, they should come to find me so I can take care of it. If somebody makes them feel outright uncomfortable, I'm gonna *really* take care of it.

If you want somebody who will say the customer is always right, grit their teeth, and bat their lashes, you have the wrong girl. It is *never* acceptable for grown men to make women feel uncomfortable, and that goes double when they're trying to do their job. I've had an incident before where I had to talk the husband of one of my team out of punching another man square in the jaw at an event, as his wife—my team member—was being treated like a piece of meat in a butcher's window. I had to convince my team member's husband that I would take care of it, and I did.

Do people call me a witch with a b when I call men out for behaving this way? What do you think? *Of course* they do. And that's OK with me. I'm cool with being *that* witch with a b.

> **It is never OK to be made to feel objectified or lesser because somebody else finds you attractive. I don't care if you're male or female; you deserve to be treated with respect.**

None of us choose the way we look in life. Because I'm blonde and I tend to smile a lot, people often refer to me as a cheerleader. This is ironic in itself; as we discussed previously, I firmly believe that self-encouragement is an inside job. You want me to be your cheerleader? I'll observe your wins and internally think "great job," but I'm not going to be on the sidelines yelling for you throughout your day. I have enough on my own slate to be dealing with. Set your own goals and motivate yourself.

That's on them though. I let it slide off my back. I know my value, and it isn't in being a cheerleader. You need to do the same. No matter what list of values you draw up, people will throw you curveballs throughout your life. They can't take your value away unless you let them.

Besides, what comes across as offensive isn't *always* meant that way. Sometimes there are cultural barriers that, as the CEO of an international business, I need to respect and be aware of. Something that looks derogatory by American standards may not be meant that way. Certain terminology doesn't mean the same thing to an overseas individual as it does to us.

Naturally, though, there will be times where it's a little much. Understanding has its limits, and there are times that I need to say, "Please do not call me that. My name is Laura, and I would appreciate it if you would address me by my name from now on."

It's very rare that people do not understand that they've ruffled feathers in this situation. If they apologize, you can explain that it's all fine and move on. There's no point in holding a grudge in that situation. It's a cultural difference, and if you can move past it, you can still enjoy a successful business relationship without sacrificing your dignity or personal values.

Your Value Doesn't Come with a Discount Coupon

Earlier this year, a competitor lowered their rates. Such is the way of the modern world, and people immediately started to reach out to me, telling me how this rival CEO was much smarter than me and asking when I would lower our rates to remain competitive. I told every single one of these people the same thing—"Go on over there. We'll see you soon."

I do not lower rates for anybody. This business isn't a race to the bottom, and I'm not selling used cars. People sometimes try to claim they know I'm lowering rates for other people, but when challenged to provide evidence of this, they can never do so. If a customer doesn't feel like we're offering value, I want to know about it. If they have a good argument, I want to be able to fix it. If they're just chancing their luck, they're more than welcome to see if the grass is greener with our competitors.

Now I hate to say I told you so, but almost every single one of those customers comes rushing back. Some of them messaged me about rates upon their return, but I just point out that we offer value, and we're legally compliant in every country that we do business in. That's *expensive*, but it's part of the value that we offer. I know what steps my competitors are skipping, and I know that's a dangerous game to play.

I always think that if you only have the budget for lemonade, don't go to a champagne bar. That doesn't have to be a bad thing. Lemonade can taste great when it means you're not going into debt to pay for it. Wait a while and drink lemonade for long enough, and you'll also save enough money to visit that champagne bar eventually. Your glass of bubbly will taste pretty sweet if you've earned it.

In addition to this, the status of our industry is constantly changing. I have talked about payment processing and the headaches that causes throughout this book, and another recent hot potato was compliance. I had people calling and emailing me in a panic saying, "Laura, we need compliance. Our projects need to be vetted."

I couldn't agree with this more. This is why JVZoo has a compliance department vetting products for our sellers. One of our competitors recently rolled out their own compliance department that looked and sounded exactly like ours. We laid the groundwork—consulting with lawyers, developing from scratch—and they took the easier route. Imitating takes a lot less effort than innovating, as does actually implementing, rather just marketing.

Even now, I have people saying they are taking their products to a competitor, as they have a compliance department. I have to point out that the notification on their products that says "in accordance with the FTC" means that we have been compliant for years. People were angry about this at first, asking who we thought we were to review their products. Now, everybody is jumping on the bandwagon.

The thing that almost makes me laugh is that our competitors aren't even performing their compliance well. On the morning that I write this, a call was escalated to me asking if I gave permission for a company to use the JVZoo trademark and logo on a product. The whole page had our trademark and copyrighted images all over it.

The product was being sold by one of our competitors that claims to have compliance procedures and to have reviewed this product, but we most certainly did not agree to the use of our copyrighted materials. Why would we?

Alas, we're also the fish in the pond that this company wants to be. This means that they let it through, hoping to turn a buck on the use of our name. We had to send a cease and desist letter to the competing company, and the owner of the product, to get it removed from sale until they completely removed any reference to JVZoo.

We don't feel the need to toot our own horn about what we do at JVZoo. The sheep will always follow the herd. After a while, they'll notice that their pockets are not lined as much and return to the business that always made them money. We let our competitors shout from the rooftops about what they have just introduced, safe in the knowledge that we are actually legally compliant, not simply claiming it. We just concentrate on providing value and doing things the right way. People like to complain in public to save face, but in private they are always looking to do business with us again.

Not for nothing, I've also heard that this cut-price competitor—with the immeasurably smarter CEO that understands the business far better than I do—has now increased their rates again. *Apparently* they lost money.

What? I already told you that I hate to say I told you so, but I'll type it right out!

Maintaining Your Value

So we have established that you are the only person who gets to take away your value. This also means that you're the only person who can maintain it. Never underestimate how important this is. Performing at your best is the simplest way to show your value, both to the outside world and yourself.

Personally, I don't just feel like I owe high performance to myself due to my own standards. I also owe it to the people who sign my paychecks and those I'm delivering a product to. This is twofold, as it applies to my role as CEO of JVZoo and as the founder of my own companies.

A strong sense of boundaries is also important. Remember, you have something to deliver in exchange for a paycheck. Let's stress this one more time—that's not a BJ. You will have reasonable expectations placed on your shoulders, though, and you need to deliver on them.

Finally, remember the difference between ego and pride.

> **While your ego is your enemy and can get in your way, having a sense of pride about the job you do is *so* important.**

Never forget that we can always be better.

I may be on one of the top rungs of the corporate ladder in my industry, but I'm criticized almost every moment of the day. I have to decipher between what is true, what I could do better, and what is just background noise. By continuing to strive for self-improvement, you'll only ever increase your value—as both an employee and a human being. If somebody else cannot see that, it's their problem.

Chapter Eleven

The Power of No

No is a powerful word. Unfortunately, it's also a four-letter word as far as some people are concerned. When a woman in business uses the word no, there is never an acceptable or accountable reason. It's because we're witches with a b and hard-nosed and relish being difficult to work with.

This means that a woman politely declining an offer will invariably send shockwaves through an industry. As we'll discuss in this chapter, that's something I have long had to accept and disassociate myself from.

Here's an example. Very recently, I decided I was no longer in a position to accept pro bono speaking engagements. I have always spoken at smaller events and venues that simply don't have the financial resources to pay me. Now, however, I simply don't have the time. Traveling and attending these events is starting to hinder my development. Time is valuable, and I really need to take a hiatus from these free gigs.

This sounds like a simple decision, and it is—for a man. In that instance, people would say, "Hey, we had a good run. Three cheers to him for working for free for so long!" In *my* case, I am already buckling up and bracing myself for the backlash. I'm experienced enough to know that it *will* come.

Previously, while my father was in the ICU of the hospital, I had to withdraw from a handful of engagements that I had previously committed to. I gave as much notice as possible and explained why I could no longer attend. When the news broke that I wouldn't be making this small number of scheduled appearances, the messages started to flood in. Let's just say that they were not empathetic letters of support.

I had already attended six conferences and events that year, before my world was turned upside down. These took place in different cities, in different countries. It's fair to say that I left a substantial footprint on live events throughout the industry in 2018. Despite this, I was immediately told that I had to stop hiding behind a computer screen, get out there, and start meeting my users face-to-face.

I understand disappointment. Maybe people were lashing out in a moment of frustration. I won't go as far as to say that I empathize or agree with that reaction though. As we've discussed in previous chapters, I consider the fact that grown adults no longer feel the need to manage their emotions to be a source of concern. All the same, people are going to do what they do. Most of the time, I let it sail over my head.

What bothered me about this instance was that the response was clearly personal, based on the fact that I'm a woman. Why do I think that? Well, take a guess at how many events the CEOs of my competitors had attended that year. If you've read the previous nine chapters of this book, you're sighing already. It wasn't even half of the number of events I had attended.

Nobody made a peep about that though. These male executives were not expected to get out into the world and meet with their users. Cut them a break, folks—they're busy ruling over their empires; they don't have the time to deal with the little people!

The moment a life-changing situation that was completely outside my control swept the rug from under my feet though? People were falling over themselves to sharpen their knives and tell me that I was hiding behind a computer screen and ducking my responsibilities to my users.

You might say that I'm paranoid. You might think the reaction to my situation was an unfortunate perfect storm. The wrong people received the wrong news at the wrong time and expressed their disappointment the only way people seem capable of in a post-Twitter world. I'll simply quote *Catch 22* in response to that—"Just because you're paranoid, it doesn't mean they aren't after you."

Experience Is Key

You may be wondering why I agreed to take unpaid speaking gigs in the first place. It's hardly like they could use the fabled, "It'll be great exposure!" line on me.

The truth is, they could. To an extent, at least. Small events are still a critical part of the process in my industry. They could be attended by new users or people who are considering entering the industry and looking for the right provider. These events were a chance to meet these people and identify the power users of the future. Because of this, I always felt obligated to attend. And generally speaking, I wanted to be there!

In addition, I was one of *very* few female speakers out there. That was something that was often used to tug on my emotional heartstrings. I lost count of how many times I was told, "Come on, Laura, you're one of the leading female figures in the industry. We need you!"

Well, that's true—I am one of the leading figures in this industry. That means I should be paid every cent a man in the same position would receive. My experience means that I am also worth more than a newbie.

I have noticed a shift in recent years, with more women being invited to speak at events. In some respects, that's admirable and progressive. What concerns me is that these decisions appear to be based on how many Instagram followers the woman in question has.

I get that, to an extent. Instagram is like its own little micro-industry. Social media is not a game that I'm well versed in. If the topic of a talk is "How to Organically Gain More Instagram Followers," I'm not the woman to host it. If it's more along the lines of "How to Grow and Improve a Business," however, you're in my house. That means I know pretty quickly when somebody has no idea what they're talking about!

I attended a talk that made me feel this way recently. I make no secret of the fact that I don't know everything. I'm always looking to learn from others. That was why I booked a seat at this talk. Another woman in business sharing her secrets and providing new insights? Sign me up!

Unfortunately, it was immediately obvious to me *why the woman* had been booked. It wasn't because she is an expert in the field. It's because she had eight hundred thousand Instagram followers.

She had clearly read a book on business. Maybe I'm selling her short—there is every chance that she listened to a podcast too. She had nothing of real value to impart though. She was unsuccessfully attempting to piece together advice that she had not applied in practice. That was frustrating for me to listen to, and it was a complete waste of my time and others'.

When I queried why this woman had been booked, it was confirmed that her Instagram following sealed the deal. OK, great. How many tickets sales did that online following translate to though? How was she monetizing that following? How was she using Instagram popularity to build her brand? Answers to these questions were not forthcoming.

This woman wasn't going to decline the opportunity to give that talk. Why should she? If somebody was willing to give her a platform, she was well within her rights to seize the opportunity. I haven't followed her since, as I would achieve nothing by doing so. Maybe she has gone on to enjoy further bookings. If that's the case, however, I'd question the wisdom of those making the bookings.

Perhaps one of the reasons I found the experience so frustrating is that it *is* possible to turn social media to your advantage. As I said, though, that's not my field of expertise. That's why in the past, I have hired somebody to manage my social media presence. I just don't have the time to master the tricks of the trade. Well, that's half the reason. The other half is that I just don't care enough to learn. Awful, but true. More times than not, social media is more about ego than real connection, and that's where it loses me. That doesn't mean there aren't great, intelligent social media account holders out there—there are. Personally, I just hate sorting through the falsified success accounts to get those who have actually achieved what their images claim.

There are incredible women out there who are using social media to build a successful brand, though they experience the same struggles as the rest of us. Take Grant Cardone's wife, Elena. She is somebody whose videos I actively enjoy watching, but in the business world, she is often presented as a plus one to Grant Cardone. She is smart and business savvy. She can hold and lead the conversation on her own merits without breaking a sweat. She is still all too often referred to as Grant Cardone's wife though.

Party Hard but Party Safe

There were definitely times earlier in my career that I was uncomfortable with saying no to people. This was most prominent when I was working in sales and I was expected to wine and dine prospective clients. I was living in New York City, and that was how things were done back then.

You'd conclude your business but find yourself still sitting in a restaurant at 10:30 at night, knowing that you had to be up again at 6:00 a.m., wondering when the ordeal was going to be over.

No, I did not want another drink—we've already had a bottle of wine, you have a wife and kids to get home to, and it's Tuesday! We've been here for hours, and I'm really not that interesting. Unfortunately, if I didn't play the game, I would have lost accounts and complaints would have been made to my manager. The moment I stopped smiling sweetly, I would have been declared obstructive and unhelpful.

I talked back in Chapter 2 about how one of my bosses expected me to go to dinner with her mortgage broker to secure her a good deal. Even before that, I was expected to attend various breakfast meetings and parties that had no relevance to my job. It was pretty obvious that she had been instructed to make sure there were some pretty girls at these events to act as gratuitous eye candy and give the men something to do between closing deals.

Eventually, I reached a point where I drew the line. I was in the office from 8: 00 a.m. to 8:00 p.m. I was done after that. I wasn't going to a hedge fund Christmas party on Wall Street because somebody had called you and said, "Hey, bring some of your girls along." I was long past the point of being impressed by table service and expensive champagne.

The sales industry really needs to leave that whole wine-and-dine culture behind, but unfortunately it's fairly universal in business. In my industry, we attend digital marketing events. I have discussed these throughout this book. Once the official event is done, there are usually drinks in the hotel or conference center. After that, it's become a tradition for male marketers to head to a strip club. I have no problem saying that I will not be there, and there is no pressure to be applied to any of my team that would also prefer not to.

I often get told, "Laura, you always go back to your hotel room after the conference. You never come to the after-party." I usually show my face at these parties, but I'll stay for one drink and make my exit after about ninety minutes. When the limo arrives to escort everybody to the next location, I make it clear that I won't be joining. To me, that's no longer business.

More importantly, I let my team know that they're all adults and can do what they want—but they are still representatives of JVZoo. In short, don't do anything that would lead to me firing you if I saw it with my own eyes.

Of course, this means that everybody reports back to me on the misdeeds of their colleagues throughout the night! Thankfully, they're only kidding. The worst thing that I recall happening was one of my guys staying out too late and falling asleep in a club. I can't say I blame him. I'd probably take a nap too. Those events can be a long day.

Mixing Business and Pleasure Rarely Ends Well

Strip clubs do not *offend* me. I know what female breasts and bottoms look like. I have my own set, after all. If a woman finds that line of work empowering, I say kudos to her. It's not my gig, but like I've said before, we all find our happiness in different ways.

Here's the thing though: guys can say until they're blue in the face that business is done in a strip club, but that's an active choice on their part. As far as I'm concerned, if you can't make a business decision without looking at T&A, it's time to review your process.

Alas, business often *is* done in strip clubs and party spots after an event. Alcohol loosens lips and limits inhibitions. In the heat of the moment, handshakes are exchanged and deals are done. That puts women who are trying to climb the ladder in a tricky spot. There is always the risk that they'll arrive at work the following morning and find that decisions were made without their input. The alternative is to tag along to these locations, potentially at the expense of their own comfort.

For good or ill, deals made in these places are usually ironclad. Nobody tries to backtrack or wriggle out of promises made the previous night. These partnerships are born of camaraderie and a desire to maintain a lifestyle. I get that. I just wonder why we can't all make friends in a restaurant! Heck, a sports bar would be fine. We can all bond over how much we hate the Patriots.

To me, the business done in a strip club is exchanging dollar bills for female nudity. That's fine. It's a transaction between consenting adults. It has little to nothing to do with digital marketing though. Well, not at JVZoo anyway. I can't speak for what happens in the offices of our competitors.

I have a female employee who is grateful I never ask her to go to these clubs. In her previous job, she was expected to be the sober one who took notes and remembered what was said and done the night before. She never minded *too* much, but she's definitely glad it's not expected of her at JVZoo.

Here's the thing. I'm not saying that predominantly male events are all bad. The fact is, I work in a male-dominated industry. I'm trying to change that, but it's going to take time. This means that men will usually outnumber women at events. It's events dominated by *predatory* males who cross lines that I have an issue with.

A woman in this industry shared a story with me that made my blood boil. She had paid to attend a mastermind event, and she was the only woman there. That wasn't an issue during the day. Ideas were flowing, she was treated with respect, and it all seemed like a great use of her time.

Dinner followed the event, and a strip club followed the dinner. She decided to head along to both. Why wouldn't she? Everything had been going swimmingly, and the flow of ideas didn't seem to be slowing down. Business was being discussed and partnerships were being forged. She wasn't going to miss out on further developments because the men decided to go to a strip club.

Things went south when she was getting ready to leave the club. She went to the bathroom, and the moment she closed the door, it reopened. One of the men from the mastermind and dinner had followed her there. All kinds of lines had been crossed—lines that only get crossed when you do business in strip clubs.

That would not have happened at the conference center. It would not have happened in the restaurant. It's what happens when partying overtakes business. A heady brew of decadence builds to a head, boundaries disappear, and things get physical.

This woman now has an issue. She does not want to be included in anything to do with this man, regardless of the time of day or setting. She does not feel safe or comfortable. This obviously hinders her ability to do business. She can't complain either though. That invites the questions that send a shiver down the spine of every woman. "Did that *really* happen? She *was* at a strip club. How much champagne did she have? What was she wearing?"

For the record, I am 100 percent certain she is telling the truth. I still recall the look on her face when she told me that story. If she was making it up, she deserves an Academy Award, but again, I know she wasn't. If she's reading this now, I believe you!

I also recall attending a morning meeting with this sleazeball once. He had a Starbucks cup in his hand, but let's just say that it wasn't filled with coffee. If I were being generous, I'd say he'd taken some inspiration from the Irish for his morning pick-me-up. If that is how he starts his days, I can't even imagine the condition he finds himself in after midnight.

Privacy Is a Right

Keeping my personal life and professional life separate is very important to me. I'm cautious about what I reveal about myself, especially when it holds no relevance to business.

I'll talk about my dog. People know that I'm divorced from Chad Casselman, who still works with JVZoo, and that we remain the best of friends. It makes sense to me that people know this. It means that if somebody wants to talk negatively about one of us, they don't do it in front of the other. People are sometimes surprised that we're so defensive of one another, but that's because our differences of opinion have nothing to do with business.

I'll talk about the importance of saving money and being prepared for a rainy day, because life can blindside you. I may even mention that I know this from experience, having suffered a serious medical setback a decade ago, without going into detail. I also mentioned my dad's illness last year, as it could have impacted my ability to attend meetings and functions, as we've already covered.

Beyond that, people don't need to know about my personal life. I'm not running a lifestyle blog. I'm running an affiliate network and a marketing firm. Neither of those has anything to do with who Laura Casselman is after 6:00 p.m. Ask me how I streamline businesses in a corporate setting, and I'll happily talk for hours. Just don't ask me how I plan to spend my Sunday afternoon. That's a rare occasion that I'm off the clock, and it holds no relevance to my business relationships.

This has given me a reputation for not going out within the industry. I'm not regarded as a party animal. I'll meet people for dinner and cocktails, but I'm not interested in being seen at parties. If I'm out at an event, I'll stick to one drink. Any more than that and there is the risk that I won't think clearly, and I make a point of avoiding business decisions when I'm not thinking clearly.

Thankfully, I'm not easily swayed. People know and respect this about me and don't try to twist my arm. Nobody tries to play "gotcha" with me—they know they won't be able to surreptitiously photo me at the bar at 2:00 a.m. The only time I have ever been out that late was when JVZoo hosted an event. We had to clean up afterward, and if my employees were expected to do that, I was going to pitch in too. That's how I work. I never expect my team to do something I wouldn't do myself.

Having said that, building relationships is a big part of my industry. That means that everybody at a party or event wants to buy me a drink. It's not that they're hoping to get me drunk and goad me into saying or doing something I would ordinarily avoid. It's more a case of being earmarked as the person that bought me a drink, so I'll remember them and we can talk later. It's a universal icebreaker, after all.

I head this off at the pass before a night even starts. I'll get to a venue early and pay the bartender, telling him that people will likely try to buy me drinks throughout the evening. I make it clear that if they order me a vodka tonic, I'm going to need that glass to contain sparkling water and lime.

That's not a judgment. I will do whatever I can to talk to everybody and give everybody their moment, within reason. I just made a conscious decision not to drink to excess in a business setting. There are people who I know very well and I've worked with for years, and maybe I'll upgrade to two glasses of wine around them. I never get tipsy around business associates though.

I'm not saying that I don't sometimes let my hair down and drink more than I should. I save that for when I'm around my friends and family though! When it comes to work, I have a strict limit where alcohol is concerned. I have no qualms about saying no when anybody tries to breach that, whether by accident or design.

Understanding the Power of No

We've discussed how powerful the word no can be. That means that we sometimes like to dance around or sugarcoat it. We often find ourselves saying, "Not just yet, but I'll take that into consideration for the future," or, "That's a great idea. I'll have to think about it for a while and come back to you."

I find this to be particularly important when I'm dealing with employees. My team is always coming up with great ideas. That's what happens when you hire smart people. Unfortunately, because I have an idea of where the business is headed months and even years into the future, I often cannot follow through on them.

All the same, I don't want people to feel like their suggestions are being shot down without a fair hearing. I want my employees to feel like members of a team. I've worked in companies in the past where we joked that the management meetings were held in the white castle. Us mere mortals had no reason to understand what was discussed in there and what the outcomes would be.

That's not how I like to run a company. I hire people because they are an asset to my business. If I could do everything, I wouldn't just be CEO; I'd be a developer, a finance officer, and the business support lead. I am not doing those jobs because there are people better at those jobs than me. I'll be blunt: *everybody* is a better developer than me! I understand code enough to play with it and see where things are going wrong (basically testing if I can make it do something it's not supposed to), but I have no interest in enhancing my knowledge beyond that.

If I have the time, I'll give an explanation for why I'm saying no and steer the conversation toward the way the company is pointed. That encourages somebody to get his or her thinking in line with the business vision. Having said that, I am completely comfortable with where I am, who I am, and what I need to do. To that end, I have no problem saying no. Sometimes it just saves a lot of time to get right to it.

I'm also flexible when I need to be. As CEO, I report to a board of directors. This means that I sometimes experience pushback when I have said no. In those instances, I may change my answer to something more positive. All it takes is a valid argument. Sometimes that's not forthcoming, and the conversation is more akin to, "This is the decision we have reached as a board. You can stay on the train or get off—your call."

There will always be the question of whether I support that decision. There have been discussions where I have made it clear that if the decision stands, then I'm out and will hand in my resignation. Luckily for me, it's never actually come to that! When it becomes clear how strongly I feel about something, the board will usually reconvene and reconsider.

Usually, this revolves around integrity issues. When all is said and done, I am the CEO of this company, and everything we do reflects on me. I can't pass the buck and say, "Well, guys, the board voted, so there's nothing more I can do." If I act upon their decisions, I am endorsing them. As I said, though, a negative response can be overturned with the right argument.

The Story Behind the No

I have been told no a number of times in my life. Sometimes, being rebuffed hurt like you know what. I'm experienced enough not to consider a no to be a rejection of Laura Casselman as a human being, but that didn't make a negative response easy to accept. Thankfully, I've been fortunate. I have typically been able to get an explanation for why I have been told no.

Not everybody will be willing to explain their decision-making. We live in a litigious society, and some people will always play their cards close to their chest. If a no stings particularly sharply, however, consider asking for more information. Be respectful and calm. Explain that you accept the decision and have no intention of attempting to overturn it. However, suggest that feedback may help you grow and improve in the future.

If somebody you really respect gives you a no or you seem to find your path blocked at every turn, there is nothing wrong with respectfully asking why. You may learn something you're doing wrong. There is nothing wrong with personal growth, especially when you're trying to expand your business.

Maybe you came in all guns blazing and were deemed too aggressive. So much of business is based on relationships and how we make people feel. If you make somebody on their team uncomfortable, they're unlikely to want to proceed.

Oftentimes, you may find there is one specific thing that you are blind to. You don't see it, so you don't notice that it's missing. For others, however, that's what they're looking for. Maybe your marketing campaign lacks a fundamental aspect. Perhaps you missed out on a critical piece of data that confirms that you understand how a business or industry operates. Constructive feedback makes all of us better.

Alternatively, you may have been unfortunate in your timing. Sometimes it rains for a week straight, and sometimes the sun is shining. Business is the same way. You may enjoy a lot of success turning left, but it's just bad luck that you met five consecutive businesses that are looking to turn right at this point. Timing can be a witch with a b, but we can't do anything about that. You just have to dust yourself off and prepare yourself for the next opportunity. There is *always* a next opportunity if you're prepared to look for it.

Use the Word No Carefully

Always be wary of people who use no as their default position. Some people wield negativity like a shield, as it spares them from having to actually do or achieve anything. I don't stand for that in my company. If somebody spends all day spitting out, "No. No. No. No," to every request like a giant toddler, they're gone. The same applies to my personal life too. I don't have time for that.

I have met a number of people in my personal and professional lives I feel sorry for but simply cannot be bothered with. I was recently musing to an employee of mine I've known for a decade that I have never met his wife. He told me she has already met all the people in her life she needs to.

How awful must that be? I felt terrible for her. At the age of thirty-two, she apparently knows so much about the world that she can just tap out now. If that ever happens to me, I'll probably draw a nice hot bath and reach for my hairdryer because there doesn't seem like much point in carrying on!

Don't get me wrong, I have gone through solid years where I have not met anybody who shattered my world. Every once in a while, though, you meet somebody that seems to tilt the axis on how you see things. They don't even need to be one of the greatest minds of our time. They just relate to you on a personal level that leaves you wondering how you have not been best friends forever.

I have a friend like this. I've known her for twenty years now, but the first time we met, we found each other a little off-putting. Our personalities are very similar, so we kind of canceled each other out. It was like an irresistible force meeting an immovable object.

The same thing happened again the next time we met . . . and we both realized how funny it was. Now, she's more than a friend—I feel like she is a part of my being. This means she can call me out on my crap like nobody else. We get together having not seen each other in months, pick up where we left off as though we've never been apart, and within two minutes she'll be saying, "You're not being true to yourself there, Laura. I don't know how, but I can just see it. You need to reel that in."

If you're going to close down that aspect of your life, where you meet new people and form new relationships, what's left? What is life beyond building and maintaining connections with other people? Even when that feels difficult, it's worth doing.

I have one employee in particular who is very hard to communicate with. He knows it, and the rest of the team knows it. We have found a synergy, though, which we have worked out along the way.

Unfortunately, there has been collateral damage throughout that journey. I have had to spend a lot of time apologizing on his behalf and explaining he didn't mean what he appeared to be saying—he's just so poor at communicating that it came across poorly and ticked somebody off.

Why do I go through that? Because this employee is good at what he does, and I have found a way to reach him. It would be easy to say, "No, you don't behave that way here. It's time for us to part ways." That would be cutting off my nose to spite my face though. He is *really* skilled, and his communication issues do not mean he has a bad heart or a lazy attitude.

We now figure each other out through other means. I'll text him about a business book that had a big impact on me and ask if it had the same effect on him. He'll send me a link to a podcast that he found really insightful and ask for my thoughts. It's not conventional, but it works for us. I'm not going to get rid of him unless he crosses another, entirely different line. This means that I need to keep an open mind about how to work with him.

Know Your No

Of course, it's sometimes hard to say no in business. As I said earlier, I hear great ideas all the time. Occasionally, I'll be pitched something that stops me in my tracks. These are the tough ones, because I'm faced with an ethical quandary. I know full well that this idea will not work at my company. However, I'm also aware that this is an absolutely killer idea.

I have to encourage people to shop that suggestion around elsewhere, for the sake of my conscience and their career. It would not be fair for me to let such innovation flounder. I'll fit it into the company strategy if I can, but it's not always an option.

In those cases, I'll tell an employee that they need to go and chase that dream—their idea is too good to stagnate. In all honesty, they know this already. Usually they're just bringing it to me so I'll say that and everything is above board.

Another hard and often heartbreaking time that no is necessary is when you know somebody is worth more than you can offer. A business is like a lime. It can only be squeezed so much before the juices run dry. I'm going through that right now. I have an employee who is surpassing what I can offer, and I don't have any other financial resources or positions available to offer them.

Thankfully, they probably won't leave any time soon. My company has a lot of goodwill in the bank with our employees because I offer a lot of freedoms that might be hard to come by in other companies. There's a lot of value to not having to come to the office and punch a clock. I don't care where or when work is done, as long as it's done.

Eventually, though, a price is put on that freedom. If I can't find a way to find that additional resource, I know this employee will eventually have to look elsewhere. Obviously, I won't bear them any ill will for doing so either. All I can do is hope that we can ride out the current period together and something else will arise.

Ultimately, I think saying no is a matter of understanding your why. Defining your why is like establishing your parameters in business. You need to know where you're going and how you're going to get there. Once you understand that, saying no becomes easy. If something or somebody is not serving those goals, there is no reason to dance around it or stand on ceremony.

That will come with backlash, especially as a woman. Saying no is like a woman using bad language—it leaves people clutching their pearls and gasping, even though it's fine when a man does it. You need to block out that noise. You need to know where you're going and stay the distance. You're going to say no more than you say yes.

This means you'll have to get comfortable with feeling uncomfortable. The world is changing, but it still isn't quite ready for strong, independent women that know their own mind and how to achieve their goals. The more of us there are, however, the more normal it will become. Eventually, people will be as OK with businesswomen saying, "no" as they are with businessmen using the same word. They'll understand that you were not being rude or hard-nosed. You just gave a straight answer, because you're too busy to waste time.

If people *can't* accept that? Well, that's their cross to bear. You know your truth, and you know what is important to you. The rest of the world may not be interested in giving you what you deserve, so you're going to have to carve out a place for yourself.

> ***No*** is not a four-letter word. It's one syllable that will change your life for the better, one use at a time.

Chapter Twelve

Top 15 Tips for Successfully Running Your Business

It's no secret that every business is different and faces unique challenges. However, I have fifteen fundamental pieces of advice that benefit *any* company, partnership, or entrepreneur. Whether you're a fledgling start-up or a seasoned CEO of a multinational conglomerate, these tips will help you overcome common concerns.

1. In the Beginning, Plan for the End

Nothing lasts forever, good, bad, or indifferent. If you're going into business with a partner, you may eventually want to go your separate ways. Ideally, you'll both move onto your next dream with a handshake and warm wishes. Unfortunately, humans are imperfect, and we do not live in an ideal world. The end of a business relationship can resemble a messy divorce. Arrange an exit plan at the beginning of your venture, getting legal contracts in place while you're still determined to do right by each other. This is a "Do not pass go. Do not collect $200" step. Never skip this step.

2. Know Your Numbers

Maybe you're not interested in numbers. You're creative—why dirty your hands with counting beans? That's what accountants are for, right? I see this attitude far too often with executives that don't hold a financial title, and it *never* fails to cause problems. Do not simply look at your gross revenue and assume all is well—that's not even half the story. Understand your *net* revenue. Whether in business or your personal accounts, factor in any savings, retirement or investments funds, and disposable income for vacations, eating out, Botox—whatever that may be, and know what your total expenses are. Understand the timing of your money too. Managing your cash flow boils down to knowing what income you're receiving—and *when*, remembering that outstanding invoices and money in the bank are two different things—and balancing this against how much is going out. I often receive SOS calls from business owners who had no idea they were in trouble until payments started bouncing. Over 80 percent of businesses that go under each year are profitable, however fail due to not understanding their cash flow.

3. Ask, or You'll Never Receive

Nobody else is going to look out for your best interests unprompted. That's on you. Ask questions, ask for meetings, ask for a raise. Anybody worth your time will respect you for knowing your mind and desires. If they don't—as we've discussed throughout this book, some people do not appreciate directness—find a different employer or business partner that will.

4. Know Your Objections and Crush Them

Nobody has succeeded in business without being at least a little cautious. If you're approaching potential investors or partners, they're going to have concerns about your business model. The same applies if you are asking for a raise at work. Your boss may have a reason *not* to spend more money pre-prepared. Be equally ready to explain why you deserve a loosening of the purse strings. Think of negotiation as a connect-the-dots puzzle. You start with a blank page, and you know what you want the final image to resemble. By methodically filling in those blanks, you'll create a clear picture that calms any nerves.

5. Plan an End Result and Work Backward

Some people in business are content to fly by the seat of their pants, hoping for the best if they *just keep talking*. Maybe that works for you, but it's not an approach I recommend. If you've successfully arranged a meeting, somebody is giving up their time because they're interested in what you have to say. Hold up your end of the bargain by retaining your focus, constantly steering the conversation toward the result that you want. Anything else is wasting everybody's time.

6. No Is Not a Four-Letter Word

Think that being told no is the worst thing that can happen? As we discussed in Chapter 11, that's not true. It's far worse to learn that an opportunity was available if you'd grabbed a brass ring, but you let it slip through your fingers. Get out there and pitch for what you want. If you get a no, you're free to move on and ask somebody else or rethink your approach.

7. Pay Yourself First—You're the Only Sure Thing

Jobs come and go, financial markets soar and crash, companies peak and fold. You need to ensure that you're taking care of your personal finances as much as those of your business. Every time you receive a paycheck, contribute a percentage to a savings bond or retirement plan before spending a single red cent. If you face unexpected hardship, the only person you can rely on to bail you out is you.

8. Rainy Days Are Coming. Investment Is Your Umbrella

Now that you've followed step 7, take some of these savings and start investing money. You don't need to be a Wall Street whiz to invest safely and sensibly. If you need advice, check out the book *Total Money Makeover* by Dave Ramsey. Dave speaks in plain English and explains how to get out of debt, budget for daily life, and prepare a future nest egg. There's a reason why this book has sold over five million copies.

9. Apply for Awards

You know who says they don't care about awards and they're just an ego trip that means nothing? People who do not win any. Awards strengthen your hand when negotiating a salary raise. They provide tangible evidence of the value of your name and work with your industry. Women and minorities, in particular, should always apply for awards. It's not just about the recognition of your peers either. Winning awards blazes a trail for others to follow. You may inadvertently inspire a young person who's wondering what to do with their life.

10. Fire Yourself Every Ninety Days

If you find yourself weighed down with workload and cannot keep up, maintain a diary of what you're doing. Review every ninety days and look out for any patterns. If you're losing time every day to administrative tasks, fire yourself from those jobs and delegate them—even if that means hiring an assistant. Every moment spent not building your business has a dollar value attached to it.

11. If It's Not Working, Let It Go

It's easy to get wedded to a beloved idea. If your plans are not working, though, it's time to move on. For the avoidance of doubt, that means *now*. If you're just scraping by for a prolonged period, convinced that you're one big break away from success, you're flogging a dead horse. Focus your energy elsewhere—you can return to your pet project later.

12. Speak When You Have Something to Say

Corporate America has an undying love for meetings. I, on the other hand, do not. If you're spending an entire day in the boardroom discussing your business, you're not at your desk *growing* your business. COVID-19 has changed the way we work, and one thing we can carry into a post-pandemic world is a little less time flapping our gums for the sake of being heard. Call a meeting when you need to. Otherwise, surround yourself with smart people and trust them to do their jobs without your direct involvement.

13. Your Time Is Your Own—Manage It

A successful businessperson can always make more money, but you can never reclaim lost time. Do whatever it takes to manage your schedule and capacity. Although I am the CEO of a tech company, I recommend going old-school here and using a notebook and pen. I have three running to-do lists at all times—master tasks that will not be completed that day but still need to be considered and tasks to be cleared that day and week. I do not allow myself to negotiate on those. Daily tasks are completed before I go to bed, and weekly tasks are wrapped up before I think about a break for the weekend. I break each day into three blocks.

- **Block 1** - clearing the most challenging and unappealing tasks so I have a clear head for the remainder of the day
- **Block 2** - anything that needs to be wrapped up early so others can do their jobs, like approving copy or making decisions
- **Block 3** - all other aspects of my role, like reviewing the business numbers or discussing projects with legal

I find this a really effective way to work, especially as every block I complete feels like a landmark and achievement. Learn what is best for you. The important thing is to conquer your workload without losing your mind.

14. Your Network Is Your Net Worth

Nobody achieves success single-handedly. You'll need connections, mentors, support, and advice. Get out from behind your desk to attend live events and conferences. Shake some hands, exchange business cards, and build relationships. Keep in touch by email if necessary, but better yet, write handwritten letters. If somebody remembers you were interested in their projects, they'll remember you when they need something you can offer.

15. Define Your Boundaries

If you're doing business, you will need to deal with human beings and their quirks. It's an oversimplification to say that the customer is always right. I've said before and I'll say again—sometimes the customer is a jerk. They're a jerk that pays your bills though. Define what is OK for you, your business, and your employees—choose what hills you're prepared to die on. If a customer crosses a line and you cannot salvage the relationship, fire them. Otherwise, make things right without compromising your integrity or beliefs.

Afterword

Now that we have reached the end of our journey together, I'd like to take a moment to thank you for reading this. I sincerely hope you've found this book helpful, but equally importantly, I hope you've gained some entertainment from what I've had to say. Life is too short to be preached to, and that was far from my intention when I sat down to write.

Most important of all, I hope you're feeling motivated, inspired, and ready to take on the world. The common theme throughout this book is that we're on the cusp of great things, but we're not yet here. We all need to play our part in creating a new world order. It's only in working together that we will be able to bring real change. Right now, naysayers and ignorance outnumber us. It's our job to change that.

Let's take a moment to summarize the things we have discussed throughout the preceding pages.

- **Be humble and always be ready to learn—but equally, don't apologize for self-belief and confidence.** There will be plenty of people out there who are keen to take you down a peg or two. Don't let them. Acknowledging your own inner strength and learning to like and admire your own mastery are pivotal steps on the road to success.

- **Never stand by and accept unequal treatment based on your gender, race, sexual orientation, or anything else.** Obviously, before you raise the alarm, ensure that you *are* being treated unequally. If you can say beyond a doubt that you are delivering the same level of service or performance as a colleague, however, and you're being overlooked for seemingly superfluous reasons, you don't need to stand for that. You deserve better, so get out there and find it. As long as you have paid your dues, you are not worth anything less than somebody else performing at the same level.

- **Take care of your reputation and image.** A good reputation can take a very long time to build, and it can be tricky to maintain. One careless word can bring your world crashing down around you—as can one spiteful rumor, regardless of whether it's true. Place your reputation and image on a solid footing, and ensure that you remain accountable for your actions.

- **Find what makes you happy, and dedicate yourself to that.** Just because you're good at something, it doesn't mean you're duty bound to build your life around that activity. Work to live, or live to work—that's your choice, and there is no right or wrong answer. Just don't build your entire existence around a job that makes you miserable. That's no way to live, and it will prevent you from reaching your full potential.

- **When you're passionate about something, channel that passion.** Find what you give an *F* about, and dedicate yourself to giving as many *F*s as you can. On the other hand, if something doesn't really matter to you, cut it loose. Who cares what your peers are saying and doing on their social media profiles? What does it matter that somebody else, in another industry, is apparently making more money than you? If something isn't directly related to what you're passionate about and is not connected to achieving your personal goals, filter it out. It's just distracting background noise.

· **Know where your strengths lie and build a platform on those.** Yes, it's important to understand your weaknesses and improve upon these areas of your life if you can. However, your strengths will help you achieve things, and you'll need to focus on these and be your own cheerleader. If you're too intimidated by the idea of your weaknesses to play to your strengths, you'll always be two steps behind where you could be.

· **Plan collaborations carefully.** There is always plenty to learn from others, and their skills and experience can complement your own to create an unstoppable force. Not every collaboration lasts forever, though, as people change and want different things. Before you hitch your wagon to somebody else, do your due diligence and plan a mutually agreeable exit strategy.

· **Stay calm and stay positive, as much as you can.** Life is going to throw you a range of curveballs, and you can't control that. You can control your reaction, though, especially as it pertains to how others see you. Nobody can retain a constant state of smiling serenity while the sky is falling around their ears, and you'll be regarded with suspicion if you try. Equally, though, try to keep your glass at least half full. Nobody wants to be surrounded by constant, unrelenting negativity. It drains the energy from a room like nothing else.

- **Know your value, and do not let anybody take it from you.** You have the same right to respect and safety in the workplace as anybody else. If somebody questions that, it's on them—you're entitled to call them on their sh**. You have your own lived experience, and nobody but you can tell you whether that's valid. You set the limits of your personal standards and comfort. Nobody else. If something matters to you, it matters.

- **Don't be afraid of the word no.** You're going to have to use it a lot in your business life, especially when you start to see a path opening up that contains roadblocks. You'll also hear it yourself, and sometimes that is going to suck. Treat it as a learning opportunity though. None of us achieve greatness without adversity. It won't be fun at the time, but that rejection could teach you something that changes the trajectory of your entire life.

That's it—I'm about to push the period key for the final time in this book. Thank you again for taking this journey with me. Grandma, if you're reading, sorry about all the swearing. Everybody else—this is your time to shine. Let's make this world a better place for working women everywhere.

I'm doing it. Countless other women are doing it. Now that I have pulled back the curtain, you can join the revolution. Together, we can bring equality to a world that has lacked it for far too long.

Acknowledgments

*I'm grateful beyond what I'll ever be able to say
for the women in my life who saw what I was allowed
to be & would not let me settle for that.*
Kai, Flying Edna

When I set out to write this book, I simply wanted to share business knowledge with others wanting to grow their careers. However, I quickly realized that the playing field is not equal. Men and women are made to play by completely different rules . . . it's not fair, but it is the reality. In consulting with others, it was clear that I'd have to share my own journey as a way of demonstrating that while the path to success isn't always straight, it is a path that can be traveled successfully and with joy.

For the guidance, support, lessons, the champions, and mentors that shaped my journey (and the writing of this book), I want to thank the following wonderful people:

First and foremost, my parents. From a young age, I've been a confident girl because I've always known I was loved and wildly capable. You have always told and shown me that I can do and accomplish absolutely anything as long as I'm willing to put in the work, continue to learn, and be kind to others. I've had a support system from day one because of your love and commitment to our family. I will never be able to thank you enough, but I will always try to make you proud.

Greg Porter, Jessica DeBry, Karen Happel, Keltie Knight, and my editors (Cortney Donelson and Stacey), you each know the part you played in making this book a reality and did so in the most pleasant of ways. I appreciate your ideas, feedback, edits, and am grateful for each of you.

To the Morgan James team—thank you for making me part of your team and also having me be a better person by cleaning up my language (a little).

Jenn Plotzke and Gretchen Brown, you are the best friends and inspiration this lady could ever have. For the countless mimosa-filled brunches and margarita nights, where you listened to me, heard me, loved me, and guided me, I will never be able to thank you enough. I love you ladies!

About the Author

Laura Casselman is the CEO of JVZoo. com and co-founder of Vidastreet LLC. Laura climbed the corporate ladder by mastering the rules of "the old boys club." More often than not, she beat them at their own game. She's been published in *Inc. Magazine*, *Entrepreneur*, and *SmartInsights*. When she's not busy commanding the room at speaking events around the world, she resides in Myrtle Beach, South Carolina.

A free ebook edition is available with the purchase of this book.

To claim your free ebook edition:

1. Visit MorganJamesBOGO.com
2. Sign your name CLEARLY in the space
3. Complete the form and submit a photo of the entire copyright page
4. You or your friend can download the ebook to your preferred device

Morgan James
BOGO™

A **FREE** ebook edition is available for you
or a friend with the purchase of this print book.

CLEARLY SIGN YOUR NAME ABOVE

Instructions to claim your free ebook edition:
1. Visit MorganJamesBOGO.com
2. Sign your name CLEARLY in the space above
3. Complete the form and submit a photo of this entire page
4. You or your friend can download the ebook to your preferred device

Print & Digital Together Forever.

Snap a photo

Free ebook

Read anywhere

CPSIA information can be obtained
at www.ICGtesting.com
Printed in the USA
JSHW012041270123
36944JS00001B/14

9 781636 980058